The IIA's Global Internal Audit Survey:
A Component of the CBOK Study

Measuring Internal Auditing's Value

Report III

Jiin-Feng Chen, PhD, CIA, CPA
Wan-Ying Lin, DBA

Disclosure

Copyright © 2011 by The Institute of Internal Auditors Research Foundation (IIARF), 247 Maitland Avenue, Altamonte Springs, Florida 32701-4201. All rights reserved. No part of this publication may be reproduced, stored in a retrieval system, or transmitted in any form by any means — electronic, mechanical, photocopying, recording, or otherwise — without prior written permission of the publisher.

The IIARF publishes this document for informational and educational purposes. This document is intended to provide information, but is not a substitute for legal or accounting advice. The IIARF does not provide such advice and makes no warranty as to any legal or accounting results through its publication of this document. When legal or accounting issues arise, professional assistance should be sought and retained.

The Institute of Internal Auditors' (IIA's) International Professional Practices Framework (IPPF) comprises the full range of existing and developing practice guidance for the profession. The IPPF provides guidance to internal auditors globally and paves the way to world-class internal auditing.

The mission of The IIARF is to expand knowledge and understanding of internal auditing by providing relevant research and educational products to advance the profession globally.

The IIA and The IIARF work in partnership with researchers from around the globe who conduct valuable studies on critical issues affecting today's business world. Much of the content presented in their final reports is a result of IIARF-funded research and prepared as a service to The Foundation and the internal audit profession. Expressed opinions, interpretations, or points of view represent a consensus of the researchers and do not necessarily reflect or represent the official position or policies of The IIA or The IIARF.

ISBN 978-0-89413-698-6
2/11
First Printing

Dedication

William G. Bishop III, CIA, served as president of The Institute of Internal Auditors from September 1992 until his untimely death in March 2004. With a motto of "I'm proud to be an internal auditor," he strived to make internal auditing a truly global profession. Bill Bishop advocated quality research for the enhancement of the stature and practice of internal auditing. To help enhance the future of this profession, it is vital for the profession to document the evolution of the profession worldwide.

Table of Contents

Acknowledgments vii

About the Authors ix

Foreword xi

Executive Summary xv

Chapter 1   Introduction 1

Chapter 2   Perceived Contributions of Internal Auditing and Organizational Characteristics 3

Chapter 3   The Relationship Between Characteristics of the Internal Audit Activity and Agreement with Value Statements 29

Chapter 4   Performance Measurement of the Internal Audit Activity 39

Chapter 5   Performance Measurement Methods and Perceived Contributions 45

Chapter 6   Audit Activities Performed and Perceived Contributions 47

Chapter 7   Conclusion 49

The IIA's Global Internal Audit Survey — Questions 51

The IIA's Global Internal Audit Survey — Glossary 57

The IIA Research Foundation Sponsor Recognition 61

The IIA Research Foundation Board of Trustees 63

The IIA Research Foundation Committee of Research and Education Advisors 64

Acknowledgments

The 21st century presents unprecedented growth opportunities for the internal audit profession. Advances in technology, the confluence of the Information and the Internet Age, and the sheer speed and expansion of communications capabilities have significantly accelerated the pace of globalization. Governance, risk, controls, and compliance processes within organizations have undergone significant change to manage the increasing complexity and sophistication of global business operations. All of these developments offer a huge opportunity for internal audit functions, whether in-sourced, co-sourced, or outsourced, including the potential to add even greater value to their respective organizations.

To ensure that a body of knowledge is systematically built up, developments in practice in a dynamically changing environment must be carefully monitored and continually analyzed to reveal critically important insights. Key lessons learned from the experience of the profession must constitute part of the historical record and be transmitted to current and future generations of internal audit professionals for optimal outcomes. Not only must we strive to secure a robust portrayal of the current state of the profession, but encourage practice-relevant research to inform and push the boundaries of practice.

We are fortunate that under the auspices of the William G. Bishop III, CIA, Memorial Fund, administered by The IIA Research Foundation, it is possible to undertake large-scale studies of the global internal audit profession. We sincerely appreciate Mary Bishop's passion and commitment to further the internal audit profession while honoring Bill Bishop's legacy. The inaugural Common Body of Knowledge (CBOK) survey under William Taylor's leadership occurred in 2006; this is the second iteration. Based on the responses from The IIA's Global Internal Audit Survey from 2006 and now in 2010, it is possible to compare results and perform high-level trending.

Five reports cover the full spectrum of a wide range of the survey questions (carefully designed to allow for comparison between the 2006 and 2010 survey data). These reports cover topical content from characteristics of an internal audit activity to implications for charting the future trajectory of the profession. The cooperation and sharing among the five report-writing teams representing the Americas, Asia, Europe, and the Middle East have made this project a truly global and collaborative effort.

We hope that this collection of reports describing the expected influence of major themes about, and developments in, the profession as extracted from the survey will provide a comprehensive snapshot of the profession globally, offer helpful insights and actionable intelligence, and point the way forward to maintaining the profession's continued relevance and value-added contributions.

For a large global project such as The IIA's Global Internal Audit Survey, the list of individuals to thank is quite extensive. First of all, our special thanks go to IIA Research Foundation Trustee Marjorie Maguire-Krupp who was involved at the inception of the CBOK study in the fall of 2008, and soon thereafter, retired former IIA President David Richards who, along with Michelle Scott, provided the initial leadership to this significant project.

In addition, we must acknowledge William Taylor and Leen Paape, both advisors to the CBOK 2010 study co-chairs, and the following international members of the CBOK 2010 Steering Committee, as well as the Survey Design Subcommittee and the Deliverables Oversight Subcommittee, for their guidance and significant contributions to the survey design, administration, data collection, interpretation, and topic-specific reports: Abdullah Al-Rowais, AbdulQader Ali, Audley Bell, Sezer Bozkus, John Brackett, Ellen Brataas, Edouard Bucaille, Adil Buhariwalla, Jean Coroller, David Curry, Todd Davies, Joyce Drummond-Hill, Claudelle von Eck, Bob Foster, Michael Head, Eric Hespenheide, Greg Hill, Steve Jameson, Béatrice Ki-Zerbo, Eric Lavoie, Luc Lavoie, Marjorie Maguire-Krupp, John McLaughlin, Fernando Mills, Michael Parkinson, Jeff Perkins, Carolyn Saint, Sakiko Sakai, Patricia Scipio, Paul Sobel, Muriel Uzan, R. Venkataraman, Dominique Vincenti, and Linda Yanta.

Several members of these committees must be particularly thanked for their extended participation in what became a prolonged, three-year commitment for this large-scale undertaking. Each of these individuals contributed their leadership, wealth of knowledge and experience, time, and effort to the CBOK study and deserves our deepest gratitude.

Professor Mohammad Abdolmohammadi of Bentley University was key to the 2010 data analysis and preparation of summary tables of the survey responses, as he was for the CBOK study in 2006. Professor Sandra Shelton of DePaul University must be recognized for giving the reports a smooth flow and an overall consistency in style and substance.

The survey could not have succeeded without the unstinted and staunch support of the survey project champions at The IIA institutes worldwide. At The IIA's global headquarters in Altamonte Springs, Florida, United States, many staff members, especially Bonnie Ulmer and Selma Kuurstra, worked tirelessly and provided indispensable support and knowledge. Bonnie Ulmer, IIARF vice president, David Polansky, IIARF executive director, and Richard Chambers, IIA president and CEO (who simultaneously served as executive director for most of the project), provided the necessary direction for the successful completion of the project.

Last but not least, The IIA's 2010 CBOK study component — The Global Internal Audit Survey — and the resulting five reports owe their contents to thousands of IIA members and nonmembers all over the world who took the time to participate in the survey. In a sense, these reports are a fitting tribute to the contributions made by internal audit professionals around the globe.

CBOK 2010 Steering Committee Co-chairs

Dr. Sridhar Ramamoorti, CIA, CFSA, CGAP
Associate Professor of Accountancy
Michael J. Coles College of Business
Kennesaw State University

Susan Ulrey, CIA, FCA, CFE
Managing Director, Risk Advisory Services
KPMG LLP

About the Authors

Jiin-Feng Chen, PhD, CIA, CCSA, CPA, is associate professor of accounting at National Chengchi University (Taiwan, Republic of China) where he teaches intermediate accounting and accounting information systems. He is an active participant at The Institute of Internal Auditors (Taiwan) and serves on its executive board. He is one of the main translators of The IIA's International Professional Practices Framework (IPPF) and COSO Guidance on Internal Control for Financial Reporting for IIA-Taiwan. Chen has published articles for the internal audit profession in *Internal Auditor (Taiwan)* and *Computer Auditing (Taiwan)* on topics related to internal audit quality assurance, electronic commerce, and Internet business reporting. His research focuses on the best practices of internal auditing and corporate governance. He also recently authored and taught continuing education programs in the areas of internal auditing, internal financial reporting standards, corporate governance, and internal control.

Wan-Ying Lin, DBA, is associate professor of accounting at National Chengchi University (Taiwan, Republic of China) where she teaches accounting principles, financial statement analysis, and issues on corporate earnings. She currently serves on an independent board of directors of a company listed in the Taiwan Securities Exchange Market. Her research focuses on internal auditing, corporate governance, business processes analysis, financial reporting, and the performance management and accountability for not-for-profit organizations. Lin has published articles in *Industrial Management and Data Systems, International Accountant, Journal of Management Research, Corporate Board: Role, Duties and Composition*, and journals issued in Taiwan on topics related to her research interests.

Foreword

The IIA's Global Internal Audit Survey: A Component of the CBOK Study

The 2010 IIA Global Internal Audit Survey is the most comprehensive study ever to capture the current perspectives and opinions from a large cross-section of practicing internal auditors, internal audit service providers, and academics about the nature and scope of assurance and consulting activities on the profession's status worldwide. This initiative is part of an ongoing global research program funded by The Institute of Internal Auditors Research Foundation (IIARF) through the William G. Bishop III, CIA, Memorial Fund to broaden the understanding of how internal auditing is practiced throughout the world.

A comprehensive database was developed, including more than 13,500 useable responses from respondents in more than 107 countries. The five reports derived from analysis of the survey responses provide useful information to internal audit practitioners, chief audit executives (CAEs), academics, and others to enhance the decision-making process involving staffing, training, career development, compliance with The IIA's *International Standards for the Professional Practice of Internal Auditing* (*Standards*), competencies, and the emerging roles of the internal audit activity.

- ***Characteristics of an Internal Audit Activity (Report I)*** examines the characteristics of the internal audit activity, including demographics, staffing levels, and reporting relationships.

- ***Core Competencies for Today's Internal Auditor (Report II)*** identifies and discusses the most important competencies for internal auditors. It also addresses the adequacy, use, and compliance with The IIA's *Standards*.

- ***Measuring Internal Auditing's Value (Report III)*** focuses on measuring the value of internal auditing to the organization.

- ***What's Next for Internal Auditing? (Report IV)*** provides forward-looking insight identifying perceived changes in the roles of the internal audit activity over the next five years.

- ***Imperatives for Change: The IIA's Global Internal Audit Survey in Action (Report V)*** contains conclusions, observations, and recommendations for the internal audit activity to anticipate and match organizations' fast-changing needs to strategically position the profession for the long term.

The 2010 survey builds upon the baseline established in prior Common Body of Knowledge (CBOK) studies (i.e., 2006), allowing for comparison, analysis, and trends as well as a baseline for comparison when The IIA's Global Internal Audit Survey is repeated in the future.

PRIOR IIA CBOK Studies

The IIA has sponsored five prior CBOK studies. The table on the following page compares the number of participating countries and usable questionnaire responses used in each CBOK study. While CBOK studies I through IV were offered only in English, the 2006 and 2010 surveys were available in 17 and 22 languages, respectively.

CBOK's Number of Respondents and Countries Over the Years

CBOK Number	Year	Number of Countries	Number of Usable Responses
I	1972	1	75
II	1985	?	340
III	1991	2	1,163
IV	1999	21	136
V	2006	91	9,366
VI	2010	107	13,582

The 2010 IIA Global Internal Audit Survey — Benefits to the Profession

Maximizing the internal audit function is imperative to meet the challenges of today's business environment. Globalization and the rapid pace of change have in many ways altered the critical skill framework necessary for success at various levels of the internal audit function. Internal auditing's value will be measured by its ability to drive positive change and improvement. It is imperative for internal auditing to examine current trends within the profession and thus be able to make recommendations for changes within the internal audit activity. This should help internal auditing to:

- Deliver the greatest value to its organization.
- Anticipate and meet organizations' needs.
- Strategically position the profession for the long term.

Research Teams

The following researchers, selected from the responses to the Request for Proposal, were involved in writing the reports and worked closely with Mohammad J. Abdolmohammadi (Bentley University, United States) who provided general data analysis from the 2006 and 2010 survey databases as well as additional analysis based on researchers' request.

Report I
Yass Alkafaji, Munir A. Majdalawieh, Ashraf Khallaf (American University of Sharjah, United Arab Emirates) and Shakir Hussain (University of Birmingham, United Kingdom).

Report II
James A. Bailey (Utah Valley University, United States).

Report III
Jiin-Feng Chen and Wan-Ying Lin (National Chengchi University, Taiwan, Republic of China).

Report IV

Georges M. Selim and Robert Melville (Cass Business School, United Kingdom), Gerrit Sarens (Université Catholique de Louvain, Belgium), and Marco Allegrini and Giuseppe D'Onza (University of Pisa, Italy).

Report V

Richard J. Anderson (De Paul University, United States) and J. Christopher Svare (Partners in Communication, United States).

Executive Summary

Report III focuses on measuring the value of internal auditing under dynamic business conditions and the key factors contributing to the value delivered by an internal audit activity. The value can be viewed from the perspectives of internal auditors/internal audit service providers, customers (such as the board, audit committee, senior management) and other stakeholders. This report covers the perceived value of internal audit activities by internal auditors/internal audit service providers. To understand the linkage between the performance of an internal audit activity and its perceived contribution (value), this report addresses 1) the relationship between organizational characteristics and the perceived contribution of an internal audit activity; 2) the effect of an internal audit activity's characteristics on its perceived contribution; 3) the effect of internal audit activity performance measurement methods on its perceived contribution; and 4) the relationship between the services performed by an internal audit activity and its perceived contribution.

An analysis of the survey responses revealed the following key findings:

- Most respondents believe that their internal audit activities add value to their organizations. Both independence and objectivity are viewed as key factors for internal audit activities to add value.

- While most respondents view their internal audit activity as contributing to controls, they do not to the same extent perceive it as contributing to risk management or governance.

- The results from regional comparisons indicate that there are significant differences across the seven regions in terms of the perceived contribution of internal audit activities to organizations.

- The most important factors to the perceived contribution of the internal audit activity are 1) having appropriate access to the audit committee; 2) functioning without coercion to change a rating assessment or withdraw a finding; and 3) more audit tools or technology used on a typical audit engagement.

- Compared to 2006, there appears to be a declining trend in sourcing the internal audit activity from outside the organization. The percentage of co-sourcing or outsourcing of the activity has an impact on its perceived effectiveness, measured in terms of process effectiveness, effective functioning, and sufficient organization status, rather than on the perception of the value added.

- The internal audit activity performance methods most frequently used include 1) assessment by percentage of the audit plan completed; 2) acceptance and implementation of recommendations; 3) surveys/feedback from the board/audit committee/senior management; 4) customer/auditee surveys from audited departments; 5) assurance of sound risk management; and 6) reliance by external auditors on the internal audit activity.

☐ The balanced scorecard and assurance of sound risk management/internal control methods are expected to gain importance as internal audit activity performance methods in the coming years.

This report provides insight to direct internal audit activities in delivering value to the organization to meet stakeholder expectations.

Chapter 1
Introduction

The IIA defines internal auditing as "an independent, objective assurance and consulting activity designed to add value and improve an organization's operations." In the Glossary of The IIA's *International Standards for the Professional Practice of Internal Auditing* (*Standards*), "add value" is defined as, "Value is provided by improving opportunities to achieve organizational objectives, identifying operational improvement, and/or reducing risk exposure through both assurance and consulting services."[1] This report focuses on measuring the value of internal auditing. Its purpose is to 1) conduct a global analysis[2] of 2010 survey data that is expected to shed some light on the relative use or different key performance indicators; and 2) provide useful and actionable information for practitioners from the analysis.

As reported in the 2006 survey, value indicators or methods used by the surveyed organizations in measuring the value of internal auditing include the acceptance and implementation of recommendations, assessment by customer surveys from audited departments, the number of management requests for internal assurance or consulting projects, and reliance by the external auditors on the internal audit activity. It is documented that "considerable differences exist between groups in the methods used to evaluate the value add by the [internal audit activities (IAAs)]" (CBOK Survey, 2006, pp. 197–199). The value provided by the internal audit activities can be viewed from the perspectives of internal audit service providers, customers (such as the board, audit committee, senior management), and other stakeholders. The survey only investigates the view of internal audit service providers; therefore, this report only covers the value of the internal audit activity as perceived by internal audit service providers.

This report goes a step further to focus on understanding the linkage between the performance of an internal audit activity and its perceived contribution (value). To better understand the linkage, the following issues are addressed:

- ☐ Is there a relationship between organizational characteristics and the perceived contribution of an internal audit activity?

- ☐ How do the characteristics of an internal audit activity affect its perceived contribution?

- ☐ Do ways of measuring the performance of an internal audit activity used by organizations affect the activity's perceived contribution?

- ☐ Is there a relationship between the services performed by and the perceived contribution of an internal audit activity?

---

[1] As of 2011, "add value" is defined as, "The internal audit activity adds value to the organization (and its stakeholders) when it provides objective and relative assurance, and contributes to the effectiveness of governance, risk management, and control processes."

[2] The global comparison is based on The IIA's classification of institutes into seven regions.

Measuring Internal Auditing's Value

The basic notion is that the value of an internal audit activity is determined by its usefulness to the organization. The usefulness of internal audit services is reflected by the activity's perceived contribution, which is affected by many factors, including organizational characteristics (Issue 1), the internal audit activity's characteristics (Issue 2), performance measurement of the internal audit activity (Issue 3), and the internal audit services performed (Issue 4). In addition, there are other factors (such as laws and regulations, corporate governance structure, and characteristics of survey respondents) that need to be considered in analyzing the value of internal auditing. A conceptual framework for the interrelationships between the perceived contribution (value) of internal auditing and these factors is illustrated in **Figure 1-1**.

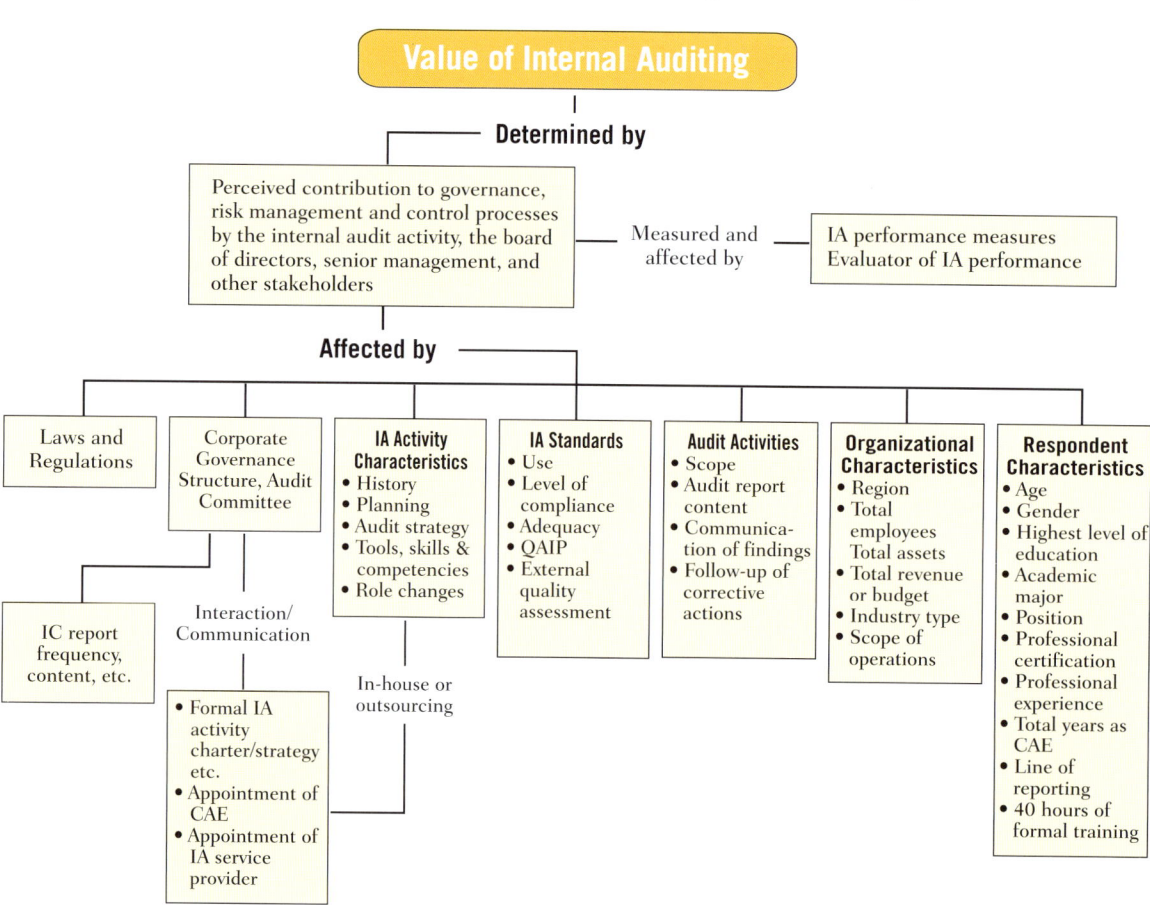

Figure 1-1: Conceptual Framework for Measuring Internal Auditing's Value

This report analyzes the relationship between organizational characteristics (such as region, industry type, and scope of operations) and the perceived contributions of internal auditing. Secondly, it examines the methods or mechanisms used by organizations to measure the performance of their internal audit activity and determines whether these methods affect the internal auditors' perceptions of their contribution. Key success factors such as the internal audit activity's organizational status, independence, strategy, staffing or competencies are identified for valuable internal audit activities. Finally, this report compares the key performance indicators used by an internal audit activity with its perceived contribution to the organization.

Chapter 2
Perceived Contributions of Internal Auditing and Organizational Characteristics

Perceived Contributions of Internal Auditing

Report III uses the perceived contribution of an internal audit activity as the proxy for its value to the organization. In the survey, one of the questions is designed to understand the respondents' perception of the contribution of their internal audit activities. The question contains 15 statements addressing the different aspects of added value of an internal audit activity to its organization. **Table 2–1** provides the respondents' level of agreement with each of the statements.

The majority of the respondents agree that their own internal audit activity:

- Is an independent objective assurance and consulting activity.
- Adds value to its organization.
- Brings a systematic approach to evaluate the effectiveness of internal controls.
- Proactively examines important financial matters, risks, and internal controls.

In addition, they agree that both independence and objectivity are key factors for their internal audit activity to add value.

In contrast, more than 30 percent of the respondents indicate that their internal audit activities do not bring a systematic approach to evaluate the effectiveness of governance processes and consider that direct access to the audit committee is not an important factor for adding value to the governance process or are neutral in their responses. However, almost 90 percent of the respondents "agree" or "strongly agree" that their internal audit activity is credible within the organization and 80 percent of them "agree" or "strongly agree" that their internal audit activities have sufficient status in the organization to be effective. Although some of the activities are less involved in the governance process, most respondents believe that they add value to their organizations.

Measuring Internal Auditing's Value Audit Activity

Table 2–1
Perceived Contributions of the Internal Audit Activity

Items		Strongly Disagree	Disagree	Neutral	Agree	Strongly Agree	Total
A1: Your internal audit activity is an independent objective assurance and consulting activity.	count	45	53	101	1,004	1,699	2,902
	%	1.6	1.8	3.5	34.6	**58.5**	100
A2: Your internal audit activity adds value.	count	31	30	163	1,389	1,278	2,891
	%	1.1	1.0	5.6	**48.0**	44.2	100
A3: Your internal audit activity brings a systematic approach to evaluate the effectiveness of risk management.	count	43	129	431	1,453	825	2,881
	%	1.5	4.5	15.0	**50.4**	28.6	100
A4: Your internal audit activity brings a systematic approach to evaluate the effectiveness of internal controls.	count	34	50	170	1,367	1,269	2,890
	%	1.2	1.7	5.9	**47.3**	43.9	100
A5: Your internal audit activity brings a systematic approach to evaluate the effectiveness of governance processes.	count	41	214	689	1,393	549	2,886
	%	1.4	7.4	23.9	**48.3**	19.0	100
A6: Your internal audit activity proactively examines important financial matters, risks, and internal controls.	count	33	113	385	1,520	835	2,886
	%	1.1	3.9	13.3	**52.7**	28.9	100
A7: Your internal audit activity is an integral part of the governance process by providing reliable information to management.	count	44	128	427	1,381	916	2,896
	%	1.5	4.4	14.7	**47.7**	31.6	100
A8: One way your internal audit activity adds value to the governance process is through direct access to the audit committee (or equivalent).	count	137	211	570	1,088	852	2,858
	%	4.8	7.4	19.9	**38.1**	29.8	100
A9: Your internal audit activity has sufficient status in the organization to be effective.	count	69	165	345	1,265	1,054	2,898
	%	2.4	5.7	11.9	43.7	36.4	100

Table 2–1
Perceived Contributions of the Internal Audit Activity (continued)

Items		Strongly Disagree	Disagree	Neutral	Agree	Strongly Agree	Total
A10: Independence is a key factor for your internal audit activity to add value.	count	40	44	139	935	1,736	2,894
	%	1.4	1.5	4.8	32.3	**60.0**	100
A11: Objectivity is a key factor for your internal audit activity to add value.	count	35	14	66	928	1,843	2,886
	%	1.2	.5	2.3	32.2	**63.9**	100
A12: Your internal audit activity is credible within your organization.	count	33	51	243	1,338	1214	2,879
	%	1.1	1.8	8.4	**46.5**	42.2	100
A13: Compliance with the *International Standards for the Professional Practice of Internal Auditing* (*Standards*) is a key factor for your internal audit activity to add value to the governance process.	count	60	183	612	1,277	758	2,890
	%	2.1	6.3	21.2	**44.2**	26.2	100
A14: Compliance with The IIA's Code of Ethics is a key factor for your internal audit activity to add value to the governance process.	count	54	111	505	1,259	963	2,892
	%	1.9	3.8	17.5	**43.5**	33.3	100
A15: Your internal audit activity meets/exceeds the requirements of The IIA's Code of Ethics.	count	46	109	569	1,356	815	2,895
	%	1.6	3.8	19.7	**46.8**	28.2	100

Most respondents believe that compliance with the *Standards* and The IIA's Code of Ethics is a key factor in adding value to the governance process and 75 percent of the respondents believe that their internal audit activity meets/exceeds the requirements of the Code of Ethics.

In summary, most respondents believe that their internal audit activities are adding value to their organizations. As expected, both independence and objectivity are viewed as key factors for internal audit activities to add value. The results also indicate that while most internal audit functions see themselves as contributing to controls, they do not to the same extent perceive themselves as contributing to risk management or governance.

The perceived contribution of the internal audit activity is measured with 15 value statements in the 2010 survey questionnaire. Based on the nature of these value statements and for the ease of discussion, the statements are classified into five sub-themes: 1) value added by the internal audit activity; 2) systematic approach to evaluate process effectiveness; 3) effective functioning of the internal audit activity; 4) adding value to governance process; and 5) organization status of an effective internal audit activity. The reasons for these groupings are as follows.

First, for an internal audit activity to add value (A2), independence (A10) and objectivity (A11) are two of the basic requirements. Furthermore, the internal audit activity contributes to the effectiveness and efficiency of governance (A5), risk management (A3), and control processes (A4). For an internal audit activity to be effective, it should provide independent objective assurance and consulting services (A1), proactively examine important financial matters, risks, and internal controls (A6), and be an integral part of the governance process by providing reliable information to management (A7). Compliance with the *Standards* (A13) and Code of Ethics (A14) is essential for an internal audit activity to add value to the governance process. Also important is an internal audit activity's direct access to the audit committee or equivalent (A8). Finally, an effective internal audit activity needs to have sufficient status (A9) and be credible within the organization (A12). Meeting or exceeding the requirements of the Code of Ethics by an internal audit activity (A15) is essential to maintaining its status and credibility. The grouping of the value statements is shown in **Table 2–2**.

Table 2–2
Sub-themes of the Value Statements Concerning Internal Audit Activity

1. Internal auditing as a value-added activity.

A2	Your internal audit activity adds value.
A10	Independence is a key factor for your internal audit activity to add value.
A11	Objectivity is a key factor for your internal audit activity to add value.

2. Systematic approach to evaluate process effectiveness.

A3	Your internal audit activity brings a systematic approach to evaluate the effectiveness of risk management.
A4	Your internal audit activity brings a systematic approach to evaluate the effectiveness of internal controls.
A5	Your internal audit activity brings a systematic approach to evaluate the effectiveness of governance processes.

3. Effective functioning of an internal audit activity.

A1	Your internal audit activity is an independent objective assurance and consulting activity.
A6	Your internal audit activity proactively examines important financial matters, risks, and internal controls.
A7	Your internal audit activity is an integral part of the governance process by providing reliable information to management.

4. Adding value to governance process.

A8	One way your internal audit activity adds value to the governance process is through direct access to the audit committee (or equivalent).

Table 2-2
Sub-themes of the Value Statements Concerning Internal Audit Activity (continued)

A13	Compliance with the *International Standards for the Professional Practice of Internal Auditing* (*Standards*) is a key factor for your internal audit activity to add value to the governance process.
A14	Compliance with The IIA's Code of Ethics is a key factor for your internal audit activity to add value to the governance process.

5. Organizational status for an effective internal audit activity.

A9	Your internal audit activity has sufficient status in the organization to be effective.
A12	Your internal audit activity is credible within your organization.
A15	Your internal audit activity meets/exceeds the requirements of The IIA's Code of Ethics.

Perceived Contributions and Regions of Work

There are regional differences in the social, economic, regulatory, and cultural environments within which organizations operate. These differences would be expected to affect the way an internal audit activity functions and its perceived contribution to the organization. This section analyzes the relationship between the respondents' perceived contribution and their regions of work based on The IIA's classification of seven regions.[3] Due to the ambiguity inherent in the Unanswered/Other category, the following analyses do not include this category. The results are presented in **Tables 2–3** through **2–9**.

Internal Auditing as a Value-added Activity

As indicated in **Table 2–3**, the Latin America and Caribbean region has the highest percentage of respondents who "strongly agree" or "agree" that their internal audit activity adds value to its organization (A2) (95.5 percent). This is followed by the United States and Canada (94.4 percent) and Western Europe (94.0 percent). The Asia Pacific region has the lowest percentage (85.2 percent) of respondents who "strongly agree" or "agree."

For statements A10 (independence) and A11 (objectivity), the differences in the levels of agreement across the regions are less significant. The Latin America and Caribbean region still has the highest percentage (96.3 percent and 98.0 percent), followed by Western Europe (93.8 percent and 97.5 percent) and the United States and Canada (91.7 percent and 96.0 percent). In addition, Europe-Central Asia and the Middle East have the lowest level of agreement on statements A10 and A11, respectively.

---

[3] Where the respondent is working for a multinational company, the survey does not investigate the regions of operation for that company. Therefore, our analysis is based only on the respondent's region of work as identified by the respondent.

Table 2-3
Regional Comparison of Value Added by the Internal Audit Activity

Region of Work:		Africa	Asia Pacific	Europe-Central Asia	Latin America and Caribbean	Middle East	United States and Canada	Western Europe	Unanswered/Other	Total
A2: Your internal audit activity adds value.										
Strongly Disagree	Col. %	2.2	1.6	0.9	0.8	0.0	1.6	0.5	0.0	1.1
Disagree	Col. %	1.5	1.6	0.9	2.0	3.4	0.9	0.5	0.0	1.0
Neutral	Col. %	5.1	11.7	6.0	1.6	5.2	3.1	5.1	14.3	5.6
Agree	Col. %	46.0	57.0	44.3	**30.2**	31.0	**42.1**	**55.3**	50.0	48.0
Strongly Agree	Col. %	45.3	28.2	47.9	**65.3**	60.3	**52.3**	**38.7**	35.7	44.2
Total	Count	137	514	336	245	58	705	882	14	2,891
	Row %	4.7	17.8	11.6	8.5	2.0	24.4	30.5	0.5	100.0
A10: Independence is a key factor for your internal audit activity to add value.										
Strongly Disagree	Col. %	2.2	1.6	1.5	0.4	1.7	1.8	1.0	0.0	1.4
Disagree	Col. %	0.7	2.0	1.5	0.4	1.7	2.1	1.2	0.0	1.5
Neutral	Col. %	4.4	6.1	7.2	2.9	5.1	4.4	4.0	14.3	4.8
Agree	Col. %	30.7	48.4	33.2	**16.7**	25.4	**31.7**	**28.2**	28.6	32.3
Strongly Agree	Col. %	62.0	42.0	56.6	**79.6**	66.1	**60.0**	**65.6**	57.1	60.0
Total	Count	137	512	334	245	59	710	883	14	2,894
	Row %	4.7	17.7	11.5	8.5	2.0	24.5	30.5	0.5	100.0
A11: Objectivity is a key factor for your internal audit activity to add value.										
Strongly Disagree	Col. %	2.2	1.6	0.9	0.8	1.7	1.7	0.7	0.0	1.2
Disagree	Col. %	0.0	1.8	0.0	0.4	0.0	0.3	0.2	0.0	0.5
Neutral	Col. %	2.2	3.1	3.9	0.8	5.1	2.0	1.6	7.1	2.3

Chapter 2: Perceived Contributions of Internal Auditing and Organizational Characteristics

Table 2-3
Regional Comparison of Value Added by the Internal Audit Activity (continued)

Region of Work:		Africa	Asia Pacific	Europe-Central Asia	Latin America and Caribbean	Middle East	United States and Canada	Western Europe	Unanswered/Other	Total
Agree	Col. %	35.6	48.7	37.0	**19.5**	25.4	**28.3**	**27.3**	28.6	32.2
Strongly Agree	Col. %	60.0	44.8	58.1	**78.5**	67.8	**67.7**	**70.2**	64.3	63.9
Total	Count	135	509	332	246	59	709	882	14	2,886
	Row %	4.7	17.6	11.5	8.5	2.0	24.6	30.6	0.5	100.0

Systematic Approach to Evaluating Process Effectiveness

Based on The IIA's definition, internal auditing helps an organization accomplish its objectives by bringing a systematic, disciplined approach to evaluate and improve the effectiveness of risk management, control, and governance processes. **Table 2–4** summarizes the respondents' assessments by region of the level at which their internal audit activity contributes to the systematic evaluation of the effectiveness of risk management, internal control, and governance processes.

Respondents across all regions indicate that their internal audit activity contributes to the systematic evaluation of internal control, followed by a slightly lower assessment of the contribution of the internal audit activity to the effectiveness of risk management. In addition, there are higher percentages of neutral responses for the statement relating to governance processes. It implies that the respondents are less confident with their contributions to the systematic evaluation of the risk management and governance processes of their organizations than the contribution of the internal audit activity to the evaluation of internal controls (**Table 2–4**).

If a mature internal audit function is defined as being one where the perceived importance of governance, risk management, and control is co-equal, then the organizational importance of internal auditing may be rated based on the three values in combination. With that in mind, **Table 2–5** presents the levels of agreement with these three statements in combination by region. Among the regions, the Middle East has the highest average level of agreement (87.6 percent), followed by Latin America and the Caribbean (84.0 percent) and Western Europe (82.5 percent). The Asia Pacific region has the lowest average level of agreement (70.5 percent).

Effective Functioning of the Internal Audit Activity

The majority of respondents from all regions "strongly agree" or "agree" that their internal audit activity is an independent objective assurance and consulting activity. The regions with the highest levels of agreement are Western Europe (95.8 percent), Latin America and Caribbean (95.5 percent), and United States and Canada (94.5 percent). (See **Table 2–6**.)

The perceived contribution of the internal audit activity in examining important financial matters, risks, and internal controls is highest among respondents from the Middle East (91.2 percent), followed by Latin America and Caribbean (89.4 percent) and Africa (86.7 percent). These regions also have the three highest levels of agreement on the contribution of the internal audit activity to providing reliable information to management (89.7 percent, 83.7 percent, and 82.4 percent). However, only 69.3 percent of the respondents from Europe-Central Asia perceive that their internal audit activity proactively examines important financial matters, risks, and internal controls, which is lower than the average percentage of 81.6 percent.

Table 2–4
Regional Comparison of Systematic Approach to Evaluating Process Effectiveness

Region of work:		Africa	Asia Pacific	Europe-Central Asia	Latin America and Caribbean	Middle East	United States and Canada	Western Europe	Unanswered/Other	Total
A3: Your internal audit activity brings a systematic approach to evaluate the effectiveness of risk management.										
Strongly Disagree	Col. %	2.2	2.2	2.7	1.2	0.0	1.1	0.9	7.1	1.5
Disagree	Col. %	5.1	5.7	5.4	2.9	5.1	5.1	3.3	0.0	4.5
Neutral	Col. %	15.3	25.0	14.7	13.9	6.8	14.2	10.5	28.6	15.0
Agree	Col. %	43.1	50.9	44.3	**44.3**	49.2	51.1	**54.8**	57.1	50.4
Strongly Agree	Col. %	34.3	16.3	32.9	**37.7**	**39.0**	28.5	**30.5**	7.1	28.6
Total	Count	137	509	334	244	59	705	879	14	2,881
	Row %	4.8	17.7	11.6	8.5	2.0	24.5	30.5	0.5	100.0
A4: Your internal audit activity brings a systematic approach to evaluate the effectiveness of internal controls.										
Strongly Disagree	Col. %	2.3	1.6	2.1	0.4	0.0	1.4	0.6	0.0	1.2
Disagree	Col. %	0.8	3.9	2.4	1.2	0.0	1.3	1.0	0.0	1.7
Neutral	Col. %	6.8	11.5	7.5	3.3	3.4	4.2	3.8	21.4	5.9
Agree	Col. %	42.4	53.3	51.5	**42.9**	45.8	40.6	**49.6**	50.0	47.3
Strongly Agree	Col. %	47.7	29.8	36.5	**52.2**	50.8	52.5	**45.0**	28.6	43.9

Table 2-4
Regional Comparison of Systematic Approach to Evaluating Process Effectiveness (continued)

Region of work:		Africa	Asia Pacific	Europe-Central Asia	Latin America and Caribbean	Middle East	United States and Canada	Western Europe	Unanswered/ Other	Total
Total	Count	132	514	334	245	59	707	885	14	2,890
	Row %	4.6	17.8	11.6	8.5	2.0	24.5	30.6	0.5	100.0
A5: Your internal audit activity brings a systematic approach to evaluate the effectiveness of governance processes.										
Strongly Disagree	Col. %	1.5	1.8	3.6	1.6	1.7	1.0	0.7	0.0	1.4
Disagree	Col. %	5.2	8.4	6.9	6.6	5.1	7.6	7.5	14.3	7.4
Neutral	Col. %	23.7	28.5	18.7	16.9	15.3	25.6	24.2	28.6	23.9
Agree	Col. %	46.7	46.3	**48.9**	**47.7**	**49.2**	48.2	49.5	50.0	48.3
Strongly Agree	Col. %	23.0	15.0	**21.8**	**27.2**	**28.8**	17.5	18.2	7.1	19.0
Total	Count	135	512	331	243	59	707	885	14	2,886
	Row %	4.7	17.7	11.5	8.4	2.0	24.5	30.7	0.5	100.0

Table 2-5
Regional Comparison of Systematic Approach to Evaluating Process Effectiveness (three statements combined)

Region of work:		Africa	Asia Pacific	Europe-Central Asia	Latin America and Caribbean	Middle East	United States and Canada	Western Europe	Unanswered/ Other	Total
A3: Your internal audit activity brings a systematic approach to evaluate the effectiveness of risk management.										
Agree	Col. %	43.1	50.9	44.3	44.3	49.2	51.1	54.8	57.1	50.4
Strongly Agree	Col. %	34.3	16.3	32.9	37.7	39.0	28.5	30.5	7.1	28.6
	Total	77.4	67.2	77.2	82.0	88.2	79.6	85.3	64.2	79.0

Table 2–5
Regional Comparison of Systematic Approach to Evaluating Process Effectiveness (three statements combined) (continued)

Region of work:		Africa	Asia Pacific	Europe-Central Asia	Latin America and Caribbean	Middle East	United States and Canada	Western Europe	Unanswered/Other	Total
A4: Your internal audit activity brings a systematic approach to evaluate the effectiveness of internal controls.										
Agree	Col. %	42.4	53.3	51.5	42.9	45.8	40.6	49.6	50.0	47.3
Strongly Agree	Col. %	47.7	29.8	36.5	52.2	50.8	52.5	45.0	28.6	43.9
	Total	90.1	83.1	88.0	95.1	96.6	93.1	94.6	78.6	91.2
A5: Your internal audit activity brings a systematic approach to evaluate the effectiveness of governance processes.										
Agree	Col. %	46.7	46.3	48.9	47.7	49.2	48.2	49.5	50.0	48.3
Strongly Agree	Col. %	23.0	15.0	21.8	27.2	28.8	17.5	18.2	7.1	19.0
	Total	69.7	61.3	70.7	74.9	78.0	65.7	67.7	57.1	67.3
Average levels of agreement	Col. %	79.1	70.5	78.6	**84.0**	**87.6**	79.5	**82.5**	66.6	79.2

Table 2–6
Regional Comparison of Effective Functioning of the Internal Audit Activity

Region of work:		Africa	Asia Pacific	Europe-Central Asia	Latin America and Caribbean	Middle East	United States and Canada	Western Europe	Unanswered/Other	Total
A1: Your internal audit activity is an independent objective assurance and consulting activity.										
Strongly Disagree	Col. %	2.9	2.3	1.5	1.2	1.7	2.0	0.7	0.0	1.6
Disagree	Col. %	2.2	2.3	2.1	1.6	1.7	1.7	1.6	0.0	1.8
Neutral	Col. %	5.8	7.2	5.7	1.6	3.4	1.8	1.9	7.1	3.5
Agree	Col. %	29.2	49.9	42.3	**24.5**	36.2	**28.9**	**30.8**	42.9	34.6
Strongly Agree	Col. %	59.9	38.2	48.5	**71.0**	56.9	**65.6**	**65.0**	50.0	58.5

Table 2-6
Regional Comparison of Effective Functioning of the Internal Audit Activity (continued)

Region of work:		Africa	Asia Pacific	Europe-Central Asia	Latin America and Caribbean	Middle East	United States and Canada	Western Europe	Unanswered/Other	Total
Total	Count	137	513	336	245	58	710	889	14	2,902
	Row %	4.7	17.7	11.6	8.4	2.0	24.5	30.6	0.5	100.0

A6: Your internal audit activity proactively examines important financial matters, risks, and internal controls.

Strongly Disagree	Col. %	2.2	1.4	3.0	0.8	0.0	0.6	0.8	0.0	1.1
Disagree	Col. %	1.5	2.5	6.3	1.6	1.8	3.3	5.5	0.0	3.9
Neutral	Col. %	9.6	12.5	21.3	8.2	7.0	10.5	15.4	21.4	13.3
Agree	Col. %	**56.6**	60.9	46.8	**53.5**	**52.6**	51.9	50.1	42.9	52.7
Strongly Agree	Col. %	**30.1**	22.7	22.5	**35.9**	**38.6**	33.8	28.2	35.7	28.9
Total	Count	136	511	333	245	57	707	883	14	2,886
	Row %	4.7	17.7	11.5	8.5	2.0	24.5	30.6	0.5	100.0

A7: Your internal audit activity is an integral part of the governance process by providing reliable information to management.

Strongly Disagree	Col. %	2.2	1.9	1.8	1.6	0.0	1.7	1.0	0.0	1.5
Disagree	Col. %	2.2	3.3	5.1	2.9	5.2	2.8	6.9	0.0	4.4
Neutral	Col. %	13.2	18.7	11.7	11.8	5.2	14.1	15.6	28.6	14.7
Agree	Col. %	**47.8**	52.0	47.3	**40.8**	**39.7**	48.1	47.5	42.9	47.7
Strongly Agree	Col. %	**34.6**	24.0	34.1	**42.9**	**50.0**	33.3	29.1	28.6	31.6
Total	Count	136	513	334	245	58	709	887	14	2,896
	Row %	4.7	17.7	11.5	8.5	2.0	24.5	30.6	0.5	100.0

Adding Value to the Governance Process

More than 84 percent of the respondents from the United States and Canada "agree" or "strongly agree" that their internal audit activity adds value to the governance process through direct access to the audit committee (or equivalent), followed by Africa (77.1 percent) and the Middle East (76.3 percent). In contrast, only 54 percent of the respondents from Asia Pacific "agree" or "strongly agree" that their internal audit activity adds value to the governance process through direct access to the audit committee or equivalent (**Table 2–7**).

This result is not consistent with the reported appropriate access of the internal audit activity to the audit committee by region. As shown in **Table 2–8**, Western Europe ranked second for the appropriate access to the audit committee (20.3 percent) and is very close to the United States and Canada (20.5 percent). In contrast, only 61.1 percent of the respondents from Western Europe indicated that their internal audit activity adds value to the governance process through direct access to the audit committee (or equivalent), which is significantly lower than that of the United States and Canada (84.6 percent). This might suggest that the audit committee does not have the same role in Western Europe that it does in the United States and Canada.

In **Table 2–7**, the percentage of respondents that "agree" or "strongly agree" that compliance with the *Standards* is a key factor for their internal audit activity to add value to the governance process was highest in Africa (87.4 percent), Latin America (85.3 percent), and the Middle East (81.4 percent). Similarly, respondents from these regions that "agree" or "strongly agree" that compliance with The IIA's Code of Ethics is a key factor for their internal audit activity to add value to the governance process was higher than any other region (87.6 percent, 86.5 percent, and 83 percent, respectively). Surprisingly, the United States and Canada has the lowest level of respondents that "agree" or "strongly agree" (62.8 percent) that compliance with the *Standards* is a key factor for their internal audit activity to add value to the governance process. Western Europe ranked last for the percentage of respondents that "agree" or "strongly agree" (70.8 percent) that compliance with The IIA's Code of Ethics is a key factor in adding value to the governance process. Considering the efforts that The IIA has made in promoting the *Standards* and the Code of Ethics in these two regions, it may be worthwhile to explore the underlying reasons for these results. It might be, for example, that these are regarded as "foundational" in the two regions and that internal audit activities have higher expectations than stated in the *Standards* and Code of Ethics. This would cause respondents to downgrade their importance.

Organizational Status of an Effective Internal Audit Activity

As indicated in **Table 2–9**, more than 80 percent of the respondents from most regions "agree" or "strongly agree" with the statements on their internal audit activity's sufficiency of status and credibility within the organization. The majority of the respondents in the Middle East (91.5 percent), Latin America (88.2 percent), and Western Europe (82 percent) "agree" or "strongly agree" that their internal audit activity has sufficient status in the organization to be effective. The same regions also ranked among the top three for the response that their internal audit activity is credible within their organization.

In general, the respondents believe that they have sufficient status and are credible in the organization. Both conditions are beneficial to the effectiveness of their internal audit activities. Asia Pacific has the lowest levels of agreement for both statements. This implies that effort may be needed to improve the status of the internal audit profession in this region.

Respondents from the United States and Canada have the highest level of agreement (85.6 percent) that their internal audit activity meets/exceeds the requirements of The IIA's Code of Ethics, followed by the Middle East (84.2 percent) and Europe and Central Asia (78.2 percent). Again, Asia Pacific has the lowest level of agreement (63.7 percent).

Table 2-7
Regional Comparison of Ways to Add Value to the Governance Process by the Internal Audit Activity

Region of work:		Africa	Asia Pacific	Europe-Central Asia	Latin America and Caribbean	Middle East	United States and Canada	Western Europe	Unanswered/ Other	Total
A8: One way your internal audit activity adds value to the governance process is through direct access to the audit committee (or equivalent).										
Strongly Disagree	Col. %	5.9	3.9	7.2	4.5	0.0	2.0	7.0	0.0	4.8
Disagree	Col. %	4.4	10.0	10.9	5.3	3.4	3.1	9.5	0.0	7.4
Neutral	Col. %	12.6	32.1	21.8	14.8	20.3	10.3	22.4	28.6	19.9
Agree	Col. %	**45.2**	35.2	31.8	32.0	**42.4**	**44.6**	36.9	50.0	38.1
Strongly Agree	Col. %	**31.9**	18.8	28.3	43.4	**33.9**	**40.0**	24.2	21.4	29.8
Total	Count	135	511	321	244	59	707	867	14	2,858
	Row %	4.7	17.9	11.2	8.5	2.1	24.7	30.3	0.5	100.0
A13: Compliance with the *International Standards for the Professional Practice of Internal Auditing* (*Standards*) is a key factor for your internal audit activity to add value to the governance process.										
Strongly Disagree	Col. %	1.5	2.0	1.5	1.6	1.7	2.8	1.9	7.7	2.1
Disagree	Col. %	0.7	4.5	3.0	3.3	5.1	10.6	7.1	0.0	6.3
Neutral	Col. %	10.4	24.9	20.1	9.8	11.9	23.8	22.5	38.5	21.2
Agree	Col. %	**42.2**	51.3	46.4	**40.2**	**40.7**	38.5	45.8	23.1	44.2
Strongly Agree	Col. %	**45.2**	17.4	29.0	**45.1**	**40.7**	24.3	22.7	30.8	26.2
Total	Count	135	511	334	246	59	709	883	13	2,890
	Row %	4.7	17.7	11.6	8.5	2.0	24.5	30.6	0.4	100.0
A14: Compliance with The IIA's Code of Ethics is a key factor for your internal audit activity to add value to the governance process.										
Strongly Disagree	Col. %	2.2	2.1	1.5	1.2	1.7	2.1	1.7	7.1	1.9
Disagree	Col. %	2.9	3.5	2.1	2.9	1.7	3.2	5.7	7.1	3.8

Table 2–7
Regional Comparison of Ways to Add Value to the
Governance Process by the Internal Audit Activity (continued)

Region of work:		Africa	Asia Pacific	Europe-Central Asia	Latin America and Caribbean	Middle East	United States and Canada	Western Europe	Unanswered/ Other	Total
Neutral	Col. %	7.3	20.3	15.6	9.4	13.6	16.0	21.8	14.3	17.5
Agree	Col. %	**39.4**	53.1	45.9	**35.9**	**32.2**	40.7	42.9	42.9	43.5
Strongly Agree	Col. %	**48.2**	20.9	34.8	**50.6**	**50.8**	38.0	27.9	28.6	33.3
Total	Count	137	512	333	245	59	708	884	14	2,892
	Row %	4.7	17.7	11.5	8.5	2.0	24.5	30.6	0.5	100.0

Table 2–8
Appropriate Access to the Audit Committee by the Internal Audit Activity

Region of work:		Africa	Asia Pacific	Europe-Central Asia	Latin America and Caribbean	Middle East	United States and Canada	Western Europe	Unanswered/ Other	Total
Do you believe that you have appropriate access to the audit committee?										
Not Answered	Col. %	79.6	83.5	84.5	85.9	86.7	78.3	76.6	76.1	80.8
Yes	Col. %	18.1	14.9	12.2	12.2	11.7	20.5	20.3	23.9	17.2
No	Col. %	2.3	1.6	3.3	1.9	1.7	1.1	3.1	0.0	2.1
Total	Count	598	2,099	1,074	1,595	412	3,231	2,798	46	11,853
	Row %	5.0	17.7	9.1	13.5	3.5	27.3	23.6	0.4	100.0

Table 2–9
Regional Comparison of Organizational Status of the Internal Audit Activity

Region of work:		Africa	Asia Pacific	Europe-Central Asia	Latin America and Caribbean	Middle East	United States and Canada	Western Europe	Unanswered/Other	Total
A9: Your internal audit activity has sufficient status in the organization to be effective.											
Strongly Disagree	Col. %	2.9	2.7	3.0	1.2	0.0	2.8	2.0	0.0	2.4
Disagree	Col. %	5.1	7.2	8.7	3.7	1.7	4.9	5.3	0.0	5.7
Neutral	Col. %	15.3	17.2	11.0	7.0	6.8	11.6	10.6	14.3	11.9
Agree	Col. %	39.4	48.1	43.0	**35.7**	52.5	43.2	**43.6**	64.3	43.7
Strongly Agree	Col. %	37.2	24.8	34.3	**52.5**	39.0	37.5	**38.4**	21.4	36.4
Total	Count	137	513	335	244	59	709	887	14	2,898
	Row %	4.7	17.7	11.6	8.4	2.0	24.5	30.6	0.5	100.0
A12: Your internal audit activity is credible within your organization.											
Strongly Disagree	Col. %	1.5	2.0	1.5	0.4	0.0	1.6	0.5	0.0	1.1
Disagree	Col. %	2.2	2.9	2.4	0.4	1.7	1.7	1.3	0.0	1.8
Neutral	Col. %	9.5	16.3	11.5	2.4	1.7	7.1	5.6	21.4	8.4
Agree	Col. %	51.1	56.1	47.7	**31.8**	48.3	42.6	**46.9**	42.9	46.5
Strongly Agree	Col. %	35.8	22.7	36.9	**64.9**	48.3	47.1	**45.8**	35.7	42.2
Total	Count	137	510	331	245	58	705	879	14	2,879
	Row %	4.8	17.7	11.5	8.5	2.0	24.5	30.5	0.5	100.0
A15: Your internal audit activity meets/exceeds the requirements of The IIA's Code of Ethics.											
Strongly Disagree	Col. %	1.5	2.2	2.7	0.8	0.0	1.4	1.4	0.0	1.6
Disagree	Col. %	5.8	4.7	3.6	4.1	0.0	2.8	3.8	7.1	3.8
Neutral	Col. %	21.2	29.4	15.5	18.7	15.8	10.1	23.4	28.6	19.7
Agree	Col. %	43.8	49.0	**57.0**	47.6	**54.4**	42.8	44.9	35.7	46.8

Table 2-9
Regional Comparison of Organizational Status of the Internal Audit Activity (continued)

Region of work:		Africa	Asia Pacific	Europe-Central Asia	Latin America and Caribbean	Middle East	United States and Canada	Western Europe	Unanswered/Other	Total
Strongly Agree	Col. %	27.7	14.7	21.2	28.9	29.8	42.8	26.5	28.6	28.2
Total	Count	137	510	335	246	57	710	886	14	2,895
	Row %	4.7	17.6	11.6	8.5	2.0	24.5	30.6	0.5	100.0

Perceived Contributions and Industry Groups

Organizations specializing or operating in different types of industry may face different kinds of technological, regulatory, and environmental challenges and opportunities. These differences, in turn, are likely to affect the way an internal audit activity functions and its perceived contribution to the organization. This section presents an analysis of the relationship between the perceived contribution and the organization's industry type based on The IIA's classification of eight industry groups. The results are presented in **Tables 2-10** through **2-14**.

Internal Auditing as a Value-added Activity

Table 2-10 indicates a high level of agreement by respondents from different industries that their internal audit activity adds value and that independence and objectivity are key factors for the internal audit activity to add value. Across all industries, statement A11 (objectivity) has the highest level of agreement.

Table 2–10
Industry Comparison of Added Value by the Internal Audit Activity

Industry Type:		Financial	Manufacturing & Construction	Public Sector/ Government	Raw Material & Agriculture	Service	Transportation, Communication, Electric, Gas, Sanitary Services	Wholesale & Retail Trade	Other	Total
A2: Your internal audit activity adds value.										
Strongly Disagree	Col. %	1.0	0.4	2.6	0.0	1.6	1.7	0.0	0.5	1.1
Disagree	Col. %	0.8	1.5	1.1	1.8	0.5	0.6	1.4	1.9	1.0
Neutral	Col. %	5.6	7.0	3.8	4.4	4.9	5.2	5.0	7.7	5.6
Agree	Col. %	45.7	51.7	51.9	41.2	45.6	47.8	49.6	51.4	48.0
Strongly Agree	Col. %	46.9	39.5	40.6	52.6	47.4	44.8	43.9	38.5	44.2
Total	Count	874	544	266	114	384	362	139	208	2,891
	Row %	30.2	18.8	9.2	3.9	13.3	12.5	4.8	7.2	100.0
A10: Independence is a key factor for your internal audit activity to add value.										
Strongly Disagree	Col. %	1.4	1.3	2.3	0.0	1.8	1.9	0.0	0.5	1.4
Disagree	Col. %	0.7	2.0	1.5	0.4	1.7	2.1	1.2	0.0	1.5
Neutral	Col. %	1.3	2.0	1.9	0.0	1.3	0.8	1.4	3.4	1.5
Agree	Col. %	26.5	39.3	32.0	30.7	31.9	34.6	34.0	35.3	32.3
Strongly Agree	Col. %	67.7	50.5	59.4	64.0	60.8	57.7	59.6	54.1	60.0
Total	Count	872	545	266	114	385	364	141	207	2,894
	Row %	30.1	18.8	9.2	3.9	13.3	12.6	4.9	7.2	100.0
A11: Objectivity is a key factor for your internal audit activity to add value.										
Strongly Disagree	Col. %	1.1	0.7	2.3	0.0	1.8	1.9	0.0	0.5	1.2
Disagree	Col. %	0.3	1.1	0.4	0.0	0.3	0.6	0.0	0.5	0.5
Neutral	Col. %	1.4	3.3	3.4	0.9	1.8	1.7	1.4	5.3	2.3
Agree	Col. %	27.3	39.4	29.9	25.7	30.4	34.2	37.1	36.4	32.2
Strongly Agree	Col. %	69.8	55.4	64.0	73.5	65.7	61.7	61.4	57.4	63.9
Total	Count	872	540	264	113	385	363	140	209	2,886
	Row %	30.2	18.7	9.1	3.9	13.3	12.6	4.9	7.2	100.0

Systematic Approach to Evaluating Process Effectiveness

Table 2–11 summarizes the respondents' levels of agreement with the three statements regarding their internal audit activity's contributions to the systematic evaluation of the effectiveness of risk management, internal controls, and governance processes. The levels of agreement (strongly agree and agree) are highest for the statement on the evaluation of internal controls (A4) across all groups, followed by risk management (A3) and governance processes (A5). Similarly, there are higher percentages of "neutral" responses for the statement relating to governance processes.

More specifically, for statement A4, the financial industry (94.4 percent) has the highest level of agreement, followed by the service industry (92.2 percent) and the raw material and agriculture industry (92.1 percent). Probably due to its nature of business and tight regulations, the financial industry leads the level of agreement for statement A3 (86.1 percent). Raw material and agriculture and service industries ranked second and third, with 83.2 percent and 78.3 percent, respectively. The levels of agreement for statement A5 are, on average, lower than those for the previous two statements. Most of the industry groups have a level of agreement below or close to 70 percent, except raw material and agriculture (78.6 percent).

Effective Functioning of the Internal Audit Activity

As indicated in **Table 2–12**, most of the respondents from all industry groups "strongly agree" or "agree" that their internal audit activity is an independent objective assurance and consulting activity (A1). The groups with the highest levels of agreement are financial (94.4 percent), service (94.3 percent), and raw material and agriculture (93.8 percent).

With respect to proactively examining important financial matters, risks, and internal controls (A6), the group with the highest level of agreement is service (85.1 percent), followed by raw material and agriculture (83.9 percent) and manufacturing and construction (82.1 percent). Financial has the top level of agreement (82.1 percent) that the internal audit activity is an integral part of the governance process by providing reliable information to management (A7), followed by service (81.3 percent) and transportation, communication, electric, gas, sanitary services (80.5 percent).

Table 2–11
Industry Comparison of Systematic Approach to Evaluating Process Effectiveness

Industry Type:		Financial	Manufacturing & Construction	Public Sector/ Government	Raw Material & Agriculture	Service	Transportation, Communication, Electric, Gas, Sanitary Services	Wholesale & Retail Trade	Other	Total
A3: Your internal audit activity brings a systematic approach to evaluate the effectiveness of risk management.											
Strongly Disagree	Col. %	0.9	1.5	2.2	1.8	1.8	2.2	0.0	1.9	1.5
Disagree	Col. %	3.0	5.5	6.0	3.5	5.0	4.4	6.5	4.4	4.5
Neutral	Col. %	10.0	20.9	14.2	11.5	14.9	16.3	17.4	19.4	15.0
Agree	Col. %	**52.6**	51.2	50.2	**52.2**	44.9	48.3	50.7	52.4	50.4
Strongly Agree	Col. %	**33.5**	20.9	27.3	**31.0**	33.4	28.7	25.4	21.8	28.6
Total	Count	871	541	267	113	383	362	138	206	2,881
	Row %	30.2	18.8	9.3	3.9	13.3	12.6	4.8	7.2	100.0
A4: Your internal audit activity brings a systematic approach to evaluate the effectiveness of internal controls.											
Strongly Disagree	Col. %	1.3	0.9	1.9	0.0	1.3	1.7	0.7	0.5	1.2
Disagree	Col. %	0.7	3.3	1.9	1.8	1.6	2.2	1.4	1.4	1.7
Neutral	Col. %	3.7	7.7	7.5	6.2	4.9	7.5	8.7	5.3	5.9
Agree	Col. %	**45.1**	50.9	52.8	**37.2**	44.7	44.0	50.0	54.1	47.3
Strongly Agree	Col. %	**49.3**	37.2	36.0	**54.9**	**47.5**	44.6	39.1	38.6	43.9
Total	Count	871	546	267	113	387	361	138	207	2,890
	Row %	30.1	18.9	9.2	3.9	13.4	12.5	4.8	7.2	100.0
A5: Your internal audit activity brings a systematic approach to evaluate the effectiveness of governance processes.											
Strongly Disagree	Col. %	1.1	1.3	3.0	0.9	1.3	1.7	1.4	1.0	1.4
Disagree	Col. %	6.8	8.1	6.0	4.5	8.6	7.5	8.7	8.7	7.4
Neutral	Col. %	22.1	27.2	20.6	16.1	26.3	21.9	26.8	27.9	23.9
Agree	Col. %	**49.3**	47.6	**49.1**	53.6	42.2	49.9	47.8	50.5	48.3
Strongly Agree	Col. %	**20.6**	15.8	**21.3**	**25.0**	21.6	19.1	15.2	12.0	19.0
Total	Count	872	544	267	112	384	361	138	208	2,886
	Row %	30.2	18.8	9.3	3.9	13.3	12.5	4.8	7.2	100.0

Table 2–12
Industry Comparison of Effective Functioning of the Internal Audit Activity

Industry Type:		Financial	Manufacturing & Construction	Public Sector/ Government	Raw Material & Agriculture	Service	Transportation, Communication, Electric, Gas, Sanitary Services	Wholesale & Retail Trade	Other	Total
A1: Your internal audit activity is an independent objective assurance and consulting activity.										
Strongly Disagree	Col. %	1.4	1.1	3.0	0.9	2.3	1.9	1.4	0.0	1.6
Disagree	Col. %	1.7	2.0	1.5	0.9	0.5	2.7	1.4	3.8	1.8
Neutral	Col. %	2.5	4.2	4.1	4.4	2.8	3.8	3.5	4.8	3.5
Agree	Col. %	**28.1**	43.5	36.0	**37.2**	**32.3**	32.4	43.3	37.5	34.6
Strongly Agree	Col. %	**66.3**	49.2	55.4	**56.6**	**62.0**	59.1	50.4	53.8	58.5
Total	Count	875	547	267	113	387	364	141	208	2,902
	Row %	30.2	18.8	9.2	3.9	13.3	12.5	4.9	7.2	100.0
A6: Your internal audit activity proactively examines important financial matters, risks, and internal controls.										
Strongly Disagree	Col. %	1.1	0.7	1.9	0.0	1.3	1.4	0.7	1.4	1.1
Disagree	Col. %	3.8	3.5	3.8	4.5	4.2	3.8	2.9	5.8	3.9
Neutral	Col. %	13.5	13.7	14.0	11.6	9.4	14.3	15.8	15.9	13.3
Agree	Col. %	50.6	**55.0**	54.7	**49.1**	**51.7**	53.8	54.7	52.9	52.7
Strongly Agree	Col. %	30.9	**27.1**	25.7	**34.8**	**33.4**	26.6	25.9	24.0	28.9
Total	Count	873	542	265	112	383	364	139	208	2,886
	Row %	30.2	18.8	9.2	3.9	13.3	12.6	4.8	7.2	100.0
A7: Your internal audit activity is an integral part of the governance process by providing reliable information to management.										
Strongly Disagree	Col. %	1.6	0.2	2.3	0.9	2.8	1.7	0.0	2.4	1.5
Disagree	Col. %	4.4	4.4	4.5	5.3	3.4	5.0	5.0	4.8	4.4
Neutral	Col. %	11.9	20.0	16.9	15.9	12.4	12.9	17.7	14.8	14.7
Agree	Col. %	**45.9**	49.0	45.5	40.7	**50.6**	**50.7**	46.8	48.3	47.7
Strongly Agree	Col. %	**36.2**	26.4	30.8	37.2	**30.7**	**29.8**	30.5	29.7	31.6
Total	Count	872	545	266	113	387	363	141	209	2,896
	Row %	30.1	18.8	9.2	3.9	13.4	12.5	4.9	7.2	100.0

Adding Value to the Governance Process

Table 2–13 presents the industry comparison of the ways of adding value to the governance process. raw material and agriculture has the highest level of agreement (77.9 percent) on statement A8, followed by financial (73.2 percent) and wholesale and retail trade (69.5 percent). On the other hand, public sector/government (55.3 percent) has the lowest percentage, possibly because the audit committee (or equivalent) is not as common in this group.

As for statement A13, the groups with the highest levels of agreement are public sector/government (74.7 percent), raw material and agriculture (73.7 percent), and financial (72.3 percent). The public sector/government respondents also show the highest level of agreement (81.9 percent) on statement A14.

Organizational Status of an Effective Internal Audit Activity

As previously indicated, more than 80 percent of the respondents "agree" or "strongly agree" with the statements regarding their internal audit activity's sufficiency of status (A9) and credibility (A12). However, for statement A9, only two groups have a level of agreement above 80 percent — financial (85.2 percent) and service (81.6 percent). This implies that the internal audit activities from other industry groups may not have the organizational status that they would like to have. Nevertheless, most of the respondents from all the industry groups "agree" or "strongly agree" that their internal audit activity adds value. Although some respondents feel that their activity does not have sufficient status, this does not necessarily affect its value to the organization.

The respondents' levels of agreement on statement A12, in general, are higher than those for statement A9. The level of agreement for all respondents is more than 80 percent and there are three groups with a level of agreement more than 90 percent — service (92.4 percent), financial (91.6 percent), and wholesale and retail trade (90.1 percent). This implies that although some of the respondents feel that their internal audit activity does not have sufficient status, it is still able to maintain its credibility within the organization.

For statement A15, "Your internal audit activity meets/exceeds the requirements of The IIA's Code of Ethics," the levels of agreement for all groups are lower than 80 percent. There is room for improvement in meeting the requirements of the Code of Ethics.

Table 2-13
Industry Comparison of Ways to Add Value to the Governance Process by the Internal Audit Activity

Industry Type:		Financial	Manufacturing & Construction	Public Sector/ Government	Raw Material & Agriculture	Service	Transportation, Communication, Electric, Gas, Sanitary Services	Wholesale & Retail Trade	Other	Total
A8: One way your internal audit activity adds value to the governance process is through direct access to the audit committee (or equivalent).										
Strongly Disagree	Col. %	3.8	4.4	6.6	3.5	5.5	5.9	2.1	6.8	4.8
Disagree	Col. %	6.0	9.3	10.0	6.2	8.6	6.7	3.5	6.8	7.4
Neutral	Col. %	16.9	23.1	28.2	12.4	17.8	21.2	24.8	16.6	19.9
Agree	Col. %	**38.0**	38.1	31.7	**39.8**	36.1	38.8	**44.7**	42.9	38.1
Strongly Agree	Col. %	**35.2**	25.0	23.6	**38.1**	31.9	27.4	**24.8**	26.8	29.8
Total	Count	860	540	259	113	382	358	141	205	2,858
	Row %	30.1	18.9	9.1	4.0	13.4	12.5	4.9	7.2	100.0
A13: Compliance with the *International Standards for the Professional Practice of Internal Auditing* (*Standards*) is a key factor for your internal audit activity to add value to the governance process.										
Strongly Disagree	Col. %	1.8	2.6	2.6	0.9	2.3	1.9	2.9	1.0	2.1
Disagree	Col. %	5.6	7.9	5.3	1.8	5.2	7.4	7.1	8.7	6.3
Neutral	Col. %	20.3	25.8	17.4	23.7	20.2	18.7	22.1	21.7	21.2
Agree	Col. %	**42.9**	43.5	**43.4**	**42.1**	45.3	46.6	47.1	45.4	44.2
Strongly Agree	Col. %	**29.4**	20.3	**31.3**	**31.6**	26.9	25.3	20.7	23.2	26.2
Total	Count	872	543	265	114	386	363	140	207	2,890
	Row %	30.2	18.8	9.2	3.9	13.4	12.6	4.8	7.2	100.0
A14: Compliance with The IIA's Code of Ethics is a key factor for your internal audit activity to add value to the governance process.										
Strongly Disagree	Col. %	1.4	2.4	2.3	0.0	2.3	2.2	2.1	1.4	1.9
Disagree	Col. %	3.9	5.1	3.0	0.9	2.6	5.0	2.1	4.3	3.8
Neutral	Col. %	18.6	19.6	12.8	19.5	15.1	15.2	21.3	17.7	17.5
Agree	Col. %	40.6	44.8	**43.6**	45.1	**44.2**	43.6	47.5	47.4	43.5
Strongly Agree	Col. %	35.5	28.1	**38.3**	34.5	**35.8**	34.0	27.0	29.2	33.3
Total	Count	871	545	266	113	385	362	141	209	2,892
	Row %	30.1	18.8	9.2	3.9	13.3	12.5	4.9	7.2	100.0

Table 2–14
Industry Comparison of Organizational Status of the Internal Audit Activity

Industry Type:		Financial	Manufacturing & Construction	Public Sector/ Government	Raw Material & Agriculture	Service	Transportation, Communication, Electric, Gas, Sanitary Services	Wholesale & Retail Trade	Other	Total
A9: Your internal audit activity has sufficient status in the organization to be effective.										
Strongly Disagree	Col. %	2.1	1.6	4.5	1.8	2.8	3.0	2.1	1.4	2.4
Disagree	Col. %	4.6	6.6	9.1	9.6	4.9	3.6	7.8	5.2	5.7
Neutral	Col. %	8.2	14.5	12.1	11.4	10.6	13.5	15.6	17.6	11.9
Agree	Col. %	**43.0**	47.3	39.8	35.1	**46.9**	**43.4**	34.8	47.1	43.7
Strongly Agree	Col. %	**42.2**	30.0	34.5	42.1	**34.7**	**36.5**	39.7	28.6	36.4
Total	Count	873	546	264	114	386	364	141	210	2,898
	Row %	30.1	18.8	9.1	3.9	13.3	12.6	4.9	7.2	100.0
A12: Your internal audit activity is credible within your organization.										
Strongly Disagree	Col. %	1.2	0.7	1.9	0.9	1.6	1.7	0.7	0.0	1.1
Disagree	Col. %	0.7	2.4	2.6	1.8	1.6	1.9	1.4	3.8	1.8
Neutral	Col. %	6.6	12.1	10.5	10.5	4.4	9.2	7.8	9.6	8.4
Agree	Col. %	**43.8**	49.9	44.4	49.1	**46.7**	43.9	**51.8**	50.2	46.5
Strongly Agree	Col. %	**47.8**	34.9	40.6	37.7	**45.7**	43.3	**38.3**	36.4	42.2
Total	Count	867	539	266	114	383	360	141	209	2,879
	Row %	30.1	18.7	9.2	4.0	13.3	12.5	4.9	7.3	100.0
A15: Your internal audit activity meets/exceeds the requirements of The IIA's Code of Ethics.										
Strongly Disagree	Col. %	2.1	1.1	3.0	0.0	1.6	1.1	1.4	1.0	1.6
Disagree	Col. %	3.2	3.7	3.4	5.3	3.1	4.1	2.9	7.2	3.8
Neutral	Col. %	17.6	25.7	17.6	21.9	17.3	16.2	27.1	19.1	19.7
Agree	Col. %	**47.8**	47.6	43.4	43.0	**46.1**	**46.2**	50.0	47.8	46.8
Strongly Agree	Col. %	**29.4**	21.9	32.6	29.8	**31.9**	**32.4**	18.6	24.9	28.2
Total	Count	875	544	267	114	382	364	140	209	2,895
	Row %	30.2	18.8	9.2	3.9	13.2	12.6	4.8	7.2	100.0

Summary and Implications

In summary, most respondents believe that their internal audit activities are adding value to their organizations, with both independence and objectivity viewed as key factors. While most internal audit functions see themselves as contributing to controls, they do not to the same extent perceive themselves as contributing to risk management or governance.

To facilitate further analyses, the value statements of the internal audit activity are classified into five sub-themes. The results from regional comparisons indicate that there are significant differences across the seven regions in terms of internal audit activities' perceived contribution to their organizations. **Table 2–15** shows the regions with the top three levels of agreement with each value statement. Latin America and Caribbean is consistently ranked among the top three for almost all the value statements except A8, "One way your internal audit activity adds value to the governance process is through direct access to the audit committee (or equivalent)" and A15, "Your internal audit activity meets/exceeds the requirements of The IIA's Code of Ethics." The other regions with a higher number of top three rankings are the Middle East (11), Western Europe (8), and United States and Canada (6). This indicates that the internal audit activities within these four regions are perceived to be adding more value to their organizations. On the other hand, the Asia Pacific respondents' level of agreement with these value statements is, in general, among the lowest of the regions. This implies that the internal audit activities in the Asia Pacific region may need more effort to enhance their value to organizations.

Organizations in different types of industry may face different challenges and opportunities. These differences are likely to affect the way an internal audit activity functions and its perceived contribution to the organization. **Table 2–16** lists the industry groups having the top three levels of agreement with each value statement. The financial industry has the highest number (12) of top three rankings, followed by raw material and agriculture (11) and service (10).

In addition, since most industry groups are spread across different regions, the results from industry comparisons represent the averaging effect of internal audit activities from different regions. There is no industry that is consistently ranked as the lowest of the industry groups.

Table 2–15
Regions with the Top Three Levels of Agreement with Value Statements

Value statements	Top three regions ranked by the level of agreement		
	1	2	3
Internal audit as a value-added activity:			
A2	Latin America and Caribbean	United States and Canada	Western Europe
A10	Latin America and Caribbean	Western Europe	United States and Canada
A11	Latin America and Caribbean	Western Europe	United States and Canada
Systematic approach to evaluate process effectiveness:			
A3	Middle East	Western Europe	Latin America and Caribbean
A4	Middle East	Latin America and Caribbean	Western Europe
A5	Middle East	Latin America and Caribbean	Europe-Central Asia
Effective functioning of the internal audit activity:			
A1	Western Europe	Latin America and Caribbean	United States and Canada
A6	Middle East	Latin America and Caribbean	Africa
A7	Middle East	Latin America and Caribbean	Africa
Adding value to governance process:			
A8	United States and Canada	Africa	Middle East
A13	Africa	Latin America and Caribbean	Middle East
A14	Africa	Latin America and Caribbean	Middle East
Organizational status for an effective internal audit activity:			
A9	Middle East	Latin America and Caribbean	Western Europe
A12	Latin America and Caribbean	Middle East	Western Europe
A15	United States and Canada	Middle East	Europe-Central Asia

Table 2–16
Industries with the Top Three Levels of Agreement with Value Statements

Value statements	Top three industries ranked by the level of agreement		
	1	2	3
Internal audit as a value-added activity:			
A2	Raw Material & Agriculture	Wholesale & Retail Trade	Service
A10	Raw Material & Agriculture	Financial	Wholesale & Retail Trade
A11	Raw Material & Agriculture	Wholesale & Retail Trade	Financial
Systematic approach to evaluate process effectiveness:			
A3	Financial	Raw Material & Agriculture	Service
A4	Financial	Service	Raw Material & Agriculture
A5	Raw Material & Agriculture	Public Sector/ Government	Financial
Effective functioning of the internal audit activity:			
A1	Financial	Service	Raw Material & Agriculture
A6	Service	Raw Material & Agriculture	Manufacturing & Construction
A7	Financial	Service	Transportation, Communication, etc.
Adding value to governance process:			
A8	Raw Material & Agriculture	Financial	Wholesale & Retail Trade
A13	Public Sector/ Government	Raw Material & Agriculture	Financial
A14	Public Sector/ Government	Service	Raw Material & Agriculture
Organizational status for an effective internal audit activity:			
A9	Financial	Service	Transportation, Communication, etc.
A12	Service	Financial	Wholesale & Retail Trade
A15	Transportation, Communication, etc.	Service	Financial

Chapter 3
The Relationship between Characteristics of the Internal Audit Activity and Agreement with Value Statements

The internal audit activity characteristics identified as factors affecting the agreement with the value statement that the activity adds value include:

- Percentage of internal audit activity co-sourced or outsourced.

- Appropriate access to the audit committee.

- Provision of a written report on the overall internal control for use by the audit committee or senior management.

- Frequency of providing an internal audit report.

- The coercion to change a rating assessment or withdraw a finding.

- The number of audit tools or technology used on a typical audit engagement.

Internal Auditing as a Value-added Activity

The analysis (see **Table 3–1**) indicates that access to the audit committee, the coercion to change a rating assessment or withdraw a finding, and audit tools or technology used have a significant relationship with assessments that the internal audit activity adds value and that independence and objectivity contribute to this value-adding agreement. This relationship, however, could not be found with respect to the provision of a written internal control report or the frequency of providing such a report. The results therefore imply that fostering a coercion-free, tools-rich working environment for the internal auditors may enhance their belief that the internal audit activity adds value to the organization.

The co-sourcing or outsourcing percentage of the internal audit activity, with the exception of the 51-74 percent category, is positively and significantly related to the statement that the internal audit activity adds value and that it is objectivity, rather than independence, that contributes to such value-adding perception. The higher the degree of internal audit activity performed by staff sourced from outside the auditee organizations the higher the proportion of agreement with the statement that objectivity is a contributor to the perceived value of the internal audit activity (96 percent, 96.6 percent, 89.6 percent, 97 percent, respectively, for the four categories and in that order).

Table 3–1
Factors Affecting the Agreement with the Value Statement: The Internal Audit Activity Adds Value

		colspan="7"	Adds value (A2)	colspan="7"	Independence (A10)	colspan="7"	Objectivity (A11)
		colspan="2" DISAGREE	colspan="2" NEUTRAL	AGREE		colspan="2" DISAGREE	colspan="2" NEUTRAL	AGREE		colspan="2" DISAGREE	colspan="2" NEUTRAL	AGREE	
		count	%	count	%	count	%	Sig	count	%	count	%	count	%	Sig	count	%	count	%	count	%	Sig
Percentage of co-sourced/ outsourced	<=25%	2	2.0	12	11.9	87	86.1		3	3.0	3	3.0	94	94.0		2	2.0	2	2.0	97	96.0	
	26-50%	2	1.7	10	8.7	103	89.6		5	4.3	4	3.4	108	92.3		1	0.9	3	2.6	113	96.6	
	51-74%	4	3.8	7	6.7	94	89.5		3	2.9	9	8.6	93	88.6		3	2.8	8	7.6	95	89.6	
	>=75%	30	1.8	60	3.6	1,588	94.6		42	2.5	74	4.4	1,567	93.1		26	1.6	25	.59	1,631	97.0	
	Total	38	1.9	89	4.5	1,872	93.7	Y	53	2.6	89	4.5	1,862	92.9	N	32	1.6	89	4.5	1,936	96.5	Y
Appropriate access to audit committee	Yes	33	1.8	70	3.9	1,687	94.3		44	2.5	71	4.0	1,681	93.6		29	1.6	30	1.7	1,738	96.7	
	No	7	3.6	17	8.6	173	87.8		10	5.1	17	8.7	168	86.2		3	1.5	8	4.1	184	94.4	
	Total	40	2.0	87	4.4	1,860	93.6	Y	54	2.7	88	4.4	1,849	92.9	Y	32	1.6	38	1.9	1,922	96.5	Y
Written report on internal control	Yes	23	1.8	55	4.4	1,172	93.8		26	2.1	52	4.2	1,175	93.8		20	1.6	22	1.8	1,214	96.7	
	No	17	2.3	33	4.5	688	93.2		28	3.8	38	5.1	675	91.1		12	1.6	17	2.3	710	96.1	
	Total	40	2.0	88	4.4	1,860	93.6	N	54	2.7	90	4.5	1,850	92.8	N	32	1.6	39	2.0	1,924	96.4	N
Frequency of providing report	On request	2	3.3	4	6.6	55	90.2		1	1.7	4	6.7	55	91.7		2	3.3	4	6.6	55	90.2	
	Annually	15	2.7	23	4.1	525	93.3		16	2.8	21	3.8	528	93.5		11	1.9	10	1.8	545	96.3	
	Periodically	8	1.2	28	4.3	616	94.5		11	1.7	28	4.3	616	94.1		8	1.2	9	1.4	639	97.4	
	Total	25	2.0	55	4.3	1,196	93.7	N	28	2.2	53	4.1	1,199	93.7	N	21	1.6	23	1.8	1,239	96.6	N
Coercion to change a rating or withdraw a finding	Yes	21	3.4	38	6.1	562	90.5		29	4.7	44	7.1	546	88.2		16	2.6	26	4.2	573	93.2	
	No	34	1.7	104	5.2	1,864	93.1		47	2.3	79	3.9	1,879	93.7		27	1.4	33	1.7	1,943	97.0	
	No ratings	6	2.4	21	8.3	227	89.4		8	3.1	15	5.9	233	91.0		6	2.4	7	2.8	241	94.9	
	Total	61	2.1	163	5.7	2,653	92.2	Y	84	2.9	138	4.8	2,658	92.3	Y	49	1.7	66	2.3	2,757	96.0	Y
No. of tools used	0	6	4.2	15	10.4	123	85.4		7	4.8	12	8.3	126	86.9		5	3.5	8	5.6	131	91.0	
	1-5	24	2.8	76	8.8	768	88.5		26	3.0	41	4.8	796	92.2		17	2.0	27	3.1	818	95.0	
	6-10	22	1.6	57	4.1	1,330	94.4		36	2.6	69	4.9	1,307	92.6		18	1.3	24	1.7	1,365	97.0	
	>11	9	1.9	15	3.2	446	94.9		15	3.2	17	3.6	442	93.3		9	1.9	7	1.5	457	96.6	
	Total	61	2.1	89	4.5	2,667	92.3	Y	84	2.9	89	4.5	2,671	92.3	Y	49	1.7	89	4.5	2,771	96.0	Y

"Y" indicates that the test result is significant at <0.05 level; "N" indicates the test result is not significant.

Systematic Approach to Evaluate Process Effectiveness

Table 3–2 reports the analysis of relationships between the internal audit activity characteristics and agreement that the activity provides systematic approach to evaluate process effectiveness. The results indicate that all factors, with the exception of the frequency of providing the internal audit report, are positively and significantly related to the level of agreement that the internal audit activity brings a systematic approach to evaluate the effectiveness of risk management, internal controls, and governance processes.

Effective Functioning of the Internal Audit Activity

The internal audit activity is perceived as effective if it is an independent objective assurance and consulting activity; proactively examines important financial matters, risks, and internal controls; and is an integral part of the governance process by providing reliable information to management. **Table 3–3** reports the analysis of the relationship between the internal audit activity characteristics and the effective function of the activity. The results indicate that all factors, with the exception of provision of written internal control report and the frequency of providing the internal audit report, are positively and significantly related to the level of agreement that the function of the internal audit activity is effective.

Adding Value to the Governance Process

Table 3–4 reports the factors related to the belief that direct access to the audit committee and compliance with the *Standards* and the Code of Ethics are key factors in adding value to the governance process. The analysis indicates that appropriate access to the audit committee, provision of written internal control report, the coercion to change a rating assessment or withdraw a finding, and the number of audit tools or technology used on a typical audit engagement are positively and significantly related to the level of agreement with such belief.

Organizational Status of an Effective Internal Audit Activity

Table 3–5 reports the analysis of factors related to the organizational status of the internal audit activity to be effective. The results indicate that percentage of co-sourced/outsourced internal audit activity, appropriate access to the audit committee, the coercion to change a rating assessment or withdraw a finding, and the number of audit tools or technology used on a typical audit engagement are positively and significantly related to the respondents' assessments that the internal audit activity has sufficient status to be effective, is credible within the organization, and meets/exceeds the requirements of The IIA's Code of Ethics.

Table 3-2
Factors Affecting the Agreement with the Statement: The Internal Audit Activity Brings a Systematic Approach

		Risk management (A3)							Internal controls (A4)							Governance process (A5)						
		DISAGREE		NEUTRAL		AGREE			DISAGREE		NEUTRAL		AGREE			DISAGREE		NEUTRAL		AGREE		
		count	%	count	%	count	%	Sig	count	%	count	%	count	%	Sig	count	%	count	%	count	%	Sig
Percentage of co-sourced/ outsourced	<=25%	10	10.1	16	16.2	73	73.7		6	6.0	16	16.0	78	78.0		19	19.2	22	22.2	58	58.6	
	26-50%	12	10.3	13	11.2	91	78.5		3	2.6	7	6.0	106	91.4		9	7.8	31	26.7	76	65.5	
	51-74%	10	9.6	11	10.6	83	79.8		5	4.8	6	5.7	94	89.5		13	12.4	22	21.0	70	66.7	
	>=75%	82	4.9	213	12.7	1,379	82.4		36	2.1	61	3.6	1,583	94.2		125	7.4	365	21.7	1,189	70.8	
	Total	114	5.7	89	4.5	1,626	81.6	Y	50	2.5	89	4.5	1,861	93.0	Y	166	8.3	89	4.5	1,393	69.7	Y
Appropriate access to audit committee	Yes	84	4.7	225	12.6	1,480	82.7		41	2.3	70	3.9	1,682	93.8		124	6.9	381	21.3	1,288	71.8	
	No	28	14.6	28	14.6	136	70.8		9	4.6	20	10.3	166	85.1		41	21.2	53	27.5	99	51.3	
	Total	112	5.7	253	12.8	1,616	81.6	Y	50	2.5	90	4.5	1,848	93.0	Y	165	8.3	434	21.9	1,387	69.8	Y
Written report on internal control	Yes	57	4.6	133	10.7	1,059	84.8		23	1.8	47	3.8	1,184	94.4		77	6.2	245	19.6	930	74.3	
	No	56	7.6	120	16.3	559	76.1		26	3.5	44	6.0	669	90.5		88	11.9	192	26.0	459	62.1	
	Total	113	5.7	253	12.8	1,618	81.6	Y	49	2.5	91	4.6	1,853	93.0	Y	165	8.3	437	22.0	1,389	69.8	Y
Frequency of providing report	On request	5	8.3	5	8.3	50	83.3		1	1.7	5	8.3	54	90.0		4	6.7	11	18.3	45	75.0	
	Annually	33	5.9	63	11.2	467	83.0		12	2.1	16	2.8	537	95.0		46	8.1	112	19.8	408	72.1	
	Periodically	22	3.4	68	10.4	562	86.2		12	1.8	27	4.1	616	94.1		29	4.5	127	19.5	496	76.1	
	Total	60	4.7	136	10.7	1,079	84.6	Y	25	2.0	48	3.8	1,207	94.3	N	79	6.2	250	19.6	949	74.3	N
Coercion to change a rating or withdraw a finding	Yes	50	8.1	89	14.4	481	77.6		28	4.5	45	7.3	545	88.2		76	12.3	140	22.7	402	65.1	
	No	100	5.0	281	14.1	1,615	80.9		46	2.3	103	5.1	1,853	92.6		144	7.2	477	23.9	1,379	69.0	
	No ratings	22	8.7	57	22.6	173	68.7		10	3.9	20	7.9	224	88.2		33	13.0	67	26.4	154	60.6	
	Total	172	6.0	427	14.9	2,269	79.1	Y	84	2.9	168	5.9	2,622	91.2	Y	253	8.8	684	23.8	1,935	67.4	Y
No. of tools used	0	15	10.4	38	26.4	91	63.2		11	7.6	25	17.2	109	75.2		24	16.6	38	26.2	83	57.2	
	1-5	77	9.0	168	19.6	612	71.4		37	4.3	82	9.5	745	86.2		111	12.9	270	31.4	479	55.7	
	6-10	66	4.7	190	13.5	1,152	81.8		26	1.8	54	3.8	1,330	94.3		103	7.3	321	22.8	983	69.9	
	>11	14	3.0	35	7.4	423	89.6		10	2.1	9	1.9	452	96.0		17	3.6	60	12.7	397	83.8	
	Total	172	6.0	89	4.5	2,278	79.1	Y	84	2.9	89	4.5	2,636	91.2	Y	255	8.8	89	4.5	1,942	67.3	Y

"Y" indicates that the test result is significant at <0.05 level; "N" indicates the test result is not significant.

Table 3–3
Factors Affecting the Agreement with the Statement: Effective Functions of an Internal Audit Activity

		Assurance & consulting (A1) DISAGREE count	%	NEUTRAL count	%	AGREE count	%	Sig	Examining financial, risk, & controls (A6) DISAGREE count	%	NEUTRAL count	%	AGREE count	%	Sig	Providing reliable information (A7) DISAGREE count	%	NEUTRAL count	%	AGREE count	%	Sig
Percentage of co-sourced/ outsourced	<=25%	3	3.0	6	6.0	91	91.0		6	6.0	23	23.0	71	71.0		11	11.0	24	24.0	65	65.0	
	26-50%	5	4.3	3	2.6	109	93.2		8	7.0	21	18.3	86	74.8		7	6.0	25	21.6	84	72.4	
	51-74%	4	3.8	4	3.8	98	92.5		5	4.8	16	15.2	84	80.0		6	5.7	14	13.2	86	81.1	
	>=75%	47	2.8	33	2.0	1,606	95.3		64	3.8	190	11.3	1,425	84.9		82	4.9	199	11.8	1,403	83.3	
	Total	59	2.9	89	4.5	1,904	94.8	Y	83	4.2	89	4.5	1,666	83.3	Y	106	5.3	89	4.5	1,638	81.7	Y
Appropriate access to audit committee	Yes	45	2.5	29	1.6	1,725	95.9		64	3.6	199	11.1	1,529	85.3		78	4.3	210	11.7	1,511	84.0	
	No	15	7.7	17	8.7	164	83.7		20	10.3	47	24.2	127	65.5		27	13.9	49	25.3	118	60.8	
	Total	60	3.0	46	2.3	1,889	94.7	Y	84	4.2	246	12.4	1,656	83.4	Y	105	5.3	259	13.0	1,629	81.7	Y
Written report on internal control	Yes	36	2.9	30	2.4	1,191	94.8		42	3.4	147	11.8	1,062	84.9		56	4.5	145	11.5	1,056	84.0	
	No	24	3.2	17	2.3	700	94.5		42	5.7	103	13.9	595	80.4		48	6.5	119	16.1	573	77.4	
	Total	60	3.0	47	2.4	1,891	94.6	N	84	4.2	250	12.6	1,657	83.2	Y	104	5.2	264	13.2	1,629	81.6	Y
Frequency of providing report	On request	3	4.9	5	8.2	53	86.9		4	6.8	5	8.5	50	84.8		2	3.3	7	11.7	51	85.0	
	Annually	15	2.7	15	2.7	536	94.7		19	3.4	75	13.3	472	83.4		25	4.4	73	12.9	468	82.7	
	Periodically	20	3.1	12	1.8	624	95.1		25	3.8	66	10.1	561	86.0		30	4.6	69	10.5	558	84.9	
	Total	38	3.0	32	2.5	1,213	94.5	N	48	3.8	146	11.4	1,083	84.8	N	57	4.4	149	11.6	1,077	83.9	N
Coercion to change a rating or withdraw a finding	Yes	37	6.0	33	5.3	552	88.8		50	8.1	91	14.7	479	77.3		56	9.0	88	14.2	476	76.8	
	No	48	2.4	51	2.5	1,912	95.1		74	3.7	256	12.8	1,667	83.5		98	4.9	287	14.3	1,620	80.8	
	No ratings	13	5.1	16	6.3	226	88.6		22	8.6	37	14.5	196	76.9		18	7.0	47	18.4	191	74.6	
	Total	98	3.4	100	3.5	2,690	93.1	Y	146	5.1	384	13.4	2,342	81.6	Y	172	6.0	422	14.7	2,287	79.4	Y
No. of tools used	0	11	7.5	13	8.8	123	83.7		14	9.7	26	17.9	105	72.4		9	6.2	41	28.1	96	65.8	
	1-5	43	5.0	41	4.7	784	90.3		50	5.8	149	17.4	660	76.8		73	8.5	175	20.3	616	71.3	
	6-10	31	2.2	37	2.6	1,345	95.2		66	4.7	170	12.0	1,176	83.3		74	5.2	173	12.2	1,166	82.5	
	>11	13	2.7	10	2.1	451	95.2		16	3.4	40	8.5	414	88.1		16	3.4	38	8.0	419	88.6	
	Total	98	3.4	89	4.5	2,703	93.1	Y	146	5.1	89	4.5	2,355	81.6	Y	172	5.9	89	4.5	2,297	79.3	Y

"Y" indicates that the test result is significant at <0.05 level; "N" indicates the test result is not significant.

Measuring Internal Auditing's Value

Table 3–4
Factors Affecting the Agreement with the Statement: Adds Value to the Governance Process

		\multicolumn{7}{c	}{Direct access to audit committee (A18)}	\multicolumn{7}{c	}{Compliance to professional standards (A13)}	\multicolumn{7}{c	}{Compliance to IIA's Code of Ethics (A14)}
		\multicolumn{2}{c	}{DISAGREE}	\multicolumn{2}{c	}{NEUTRAL}	\multicolumn{2}{c	}{AGREE}		\multicolumn{2}{c	}{DISAGREE}	\multicolumn{2}{c	}{NEUTRAL}	\multicolumn{2}{c	}{AGREE}		\multicolumn{2}{c	}{DISAGREE}	\multicolumn{2}{c	}{NEUTRAL}	\multicolumn{2}{c	}{AGREE}	
		count	%	count	%	count	%	Sig	count	%	count	%	count	%	Sig	count	%	count	%	count	%	Sig
Percentage of co-sourced/outsourced	<=25%	24	24.2	32	32.3	43	43.4		5	5.1	23	23.2	71	71.7		6	6.1	20	20.2	73	73.7	
	26-50%	28	24.0	34	29.1	55	47.0		18	15.5	18	15.5	80	69.0		10	8.6	23	20.0	84	71.8	
	51-74%	11	10.4	23	21.7	72	67.9		13	12.4	23	21.9	69	65.7		7	6.7	27	25.7	71	67.6	
	>=75%	63	3.8	192	11.4	1,423	84.8		143	8.5	334	19.9	1,203	71.6		92	5.5	274	16.3	1,316	78.2	
	Total	126	6.3	89	4.5	1,593	79.7	Y	179	9.0	89	4.5	1,423	71.2	N	115	5.7	89	4.5	1,544	77.1	N
Appropriate access to audit committee	Yes	71	4.0	215	12.0	1,508	84.1		146	8.1	352	19.6	1,296	72.2		90	5.0	295	16.4	1,410	78.6	
	No	52	26.9	58	30.1	83	43.0		33	17.0	46	23.7	115	59.3		25	12.8	46	23.6	124	63.6	
	Total	123	6.2	273	13.7	1,591	80.1	Y	179	9.0	398	20.0	1,411	71.0	Y	115	5.8	341	17.1	1,534	77.1	Y
Written report on internal controls	Yes	63	5.0	175	14.0	1,014	81.0		96	7.7	240	19.1	918	73.2		65	5.2	205	16.4	983	78.5	
	No	61	8.3	103	13.9	575	77.8		84	11.4	159	21.6	494	67.0		50	6.8	138	18.6	553	74.6	
	Total	124	6.2	278	14.0	1,589	79.8	Y	180	9.0	399	20.0	1,412	70.9	Y	115	5.8	343	17.2	1,536	77.0	Y
Frequency of providing report	On request	5	8.2	12	19.7	44	72.1		3	4.9	11	18.0	47	77.1		4	6.6	12	19.7	45	73.8	
	Annually	36	6.4	89	15.8	439	77.8		46	8.2	114	20.2	404	71.6		34	6.0	95	16.8	435	77.1	
	Periodically	24	3.7	78	11.9	552	84.4		49	7.5	114	17.4	493	75.2		29	4.4	101	15.4	525	80.2	
	Total	65	5.1	179	14.0	1,035	80.9	Y	98	7.7	239	18.7	944	73.7	N	67	5.2	208	16.3	1,005	78.5	N
Coercion to change a rating or withdraw a finding	Yes	108	17.7	125	20.5	377	61.8		71	11.5	124	20.0	424	68.5		54	8.7	105	17.0	459	74.3	
	No	203	10.3	373	18.9	1403	70.9		143	7.1	410	20.5	1,451	72.4		95	4.7	335	16.7	1576	78.6	
	No ratings	34	13.3	65	25.5	156	61.2		29	11.5	73	28.9	151	59.7		16	6.3	61	23.9	178	69.8	
	Total	345	12.1	563	19.8	1,936	68.1	Y	243	8.5	607	21.1	2,026	70.5	Y	165	5.7	501	17.4	2,213	76.9	Y
No. of tools used	0	18	12.6	44	30.8	81	56.6		11	7.5	37	25.2	99	67.4		6	4.1	33	22.8	106	73.1	
	1-5	119	13.9	224	26.2	511	59.8		95	11.0	224	26.0	542	63.0		63	7.3	206	23.8	597	68.9	
	6-10	171	12.3	240	17.2	982	70.5		115	8.2	286	20.3	1,007	71.5		76	5.4	220	15.6	1,111	79.0	
	>11	40	8.6	62	13.3	366	78.2		22	4.6	65	13.7	387	81.7		20	4.2	46	9.7	408	86.1	
	Total	348	12.2	89	4.5	1,940	67.9	Y	243	8.4	89	4.5	2,035	70.4	Y	165	5.7	89	4.5	2,222	76.8	Y

"Y" indicates that the test result is significant at <0.05 level; "N" indicates the test result is not significant.

Table 3-5
Factors Affecting the Agreement with the Statement: Organizational Status for the Internal Audit Activity to Be Effective

		Status (A9) DISAGREE count	%	NEUTRAL count	%	AGREE count	%	Sig	Credible (A12) DISAGREE count	%	NEUTRAL count	%	AGREE count	%	Sig	Meeting/exceeding IIA's Code of Ethics (A15) DISAGREE count	%	NEUTRAL count	%	AGREE count	%	Sig
Percentage of co-sourced/outsourced	<=25%	3	3.0	6	6.0	91	91.0		7	7.1	12	12.1	80	80.8		9	8.9	28	27.7	64	63.4	
	26-50%	5	4.3	3	2.6	109	93.2		6	5.2	11	9.5	99	85.3		8	6.8	25	21.4	84	71.8	
	51-74%	4	3.8	4	3.8	98	92.5		3	2.8	5	4.7	98	92.5		6	5.7	20	18.9	80	75.5	
	>=75%	47	2.8	33	2.0	1,606	95.3		35	2.1	109	6.5	1,531	91.4		67	4.0	272	16.2	1,342	79.8	
	Total	59	2.9	89	4.5	1,904	94.8	Y	51	2.6	89	4.5	1,808	90.6	Y	90	4.5	89	4.5	1,570	78.3	Y
Appropriate access to audit committee	Yes	45	2.5	29	1.6	1,725	95.9		37	2.1	106	5.9	1,645	92.0		62	3.5	294	16.4	1,438	80.2	
	No	15	7.7	17	8.7	164	83.7		14	7.2	33	16.9	148	75.9		27	13.7	49	24.9	121	61.4	
	Total	60	3.0	46	2.3	1,889	94.7	Y	51	2.6	139	7.0	1,793	90.4	Y	89	4.5	343	17.2	1,559	78.3	Y
Written report on internal control	Yes	36	2.9	30	2.4	1,191	94.8		25	2.0	84	6.7	1,140	91.3		53	4.2	219	17.5	982	78.3	
	No	24	3.2	17	2.3	700	94.5		26	3.5	55	7.5	657	89.0		37	5.0	126	17.0	577	78.0	
	Total	60	3.0	47	2.4	1,891	94.6	N	51	2.6	139	7.0	1,797	90.4	N	90	4.5	345	17.3	1,559	78.2	Y
Frequency of providing report	On request	3	4.9	5	8.2	53	86.9		0	0.0	4	6.7	56	93.3		4	6.7	14	23.3	42	70.0	
	Annually	15	2.7	15	2.7	536	94.7		13	2.3	40	7.1	510	90.6		24	4.2	90	15.9	452	79.9	
	Periodically	20	3.1	12	1.8	624	95.1		13	2.0	42	6.4	598	91.6		28	4.3	117	17.9	510	77.9	
	Total	38	3.0	32	2.5	1,213	94.5	N	26	2.0	86	6.7	1,164	91.2	N	56	4.4	221	17.3	1,004	78.4	N
Coercion to change a rating or withdraw a finding	Yes	37	6.0	33	5.3	552	88.8		30	4.9	66	10.7	519	84.4		57	9.3	125	20.3	433	70.4	
	No	48	2.4	51	2.5	1,912	95.1		44	2.2	139	7.0	1,814	90.8		77	3.8	383	19.1	1,550	77.1	
	No ratings	13	5.1	16	6.3	226	88.6		10	4.0	36	14.2	207	81.8		21	8.2	57	22.3	178	69.5	
	Total	98	3.4	100	3.5	2,690	93.1	Y	84	2.9	241	8.4	2,540	88.7	Y	155	5.4	565	19.6	2,161	75.0	Y
No. of tools used	0	11	7.5	13	8.8	123	83.7		6	4.2	22	15.4	115	80.4		13	9.0	44	30.3	88	60.7	
	1-5	43	5.0	41	4.7	784	90.3		44	5.1	117	13.6	702	81.3		64	7.4	246	28.4	556	64.2	
	6-10	31	2.2	37	2.6	1,345	95.2		25	1.8	91	6.5	1,286	91.7		65	4.6	232	16.4	1,114	79.0	
	>11	13	2.7	10	2.1	451	95.2		9	1.9	13	2.8	449	95.3		13	2.8	47	9.9	413	87.3	
	Total	98	3.4	89	4.5	2,703	93.1	Y	84	2.9	89	4.5	2,552	88.6	Y	155	5.4	89	4.5	2,171	75.0	Y

"Y" indicates that the test result is significant at <0.05 level; "N" indicates the test result is not significant.

Summary and Implications

Based on the nature of the value statements asked in the survey, the value statements are divided into five groupings to facilitate our analyses: 1) value added by the internal audit activity; 2) systematic approach to evaluate process effectiveness; 3) effective functioning of the internal audit activity; 4) adding value to the governance process; and 5) organization status of an effective internal audit activity. The investigation of the relationship between characteristics of the internal audit activity and the level of agreement with the grouped value statements regarding the activity was then performed. **Table 3–6** summarizes the most and the least important factors of the internal audit activity characteristics affecting the perceived contribution of the activity based upon the significance of the findings from **Tables 3–1** through **3–5**.

Table 3–6
Summary of Factors Affecting the Agreement with the Value Statements

IAA characteristics	IAA adds value	Process effectiveness	Effective functioning	Add value to governance process	Organization status
Co-sourced/outsourced		V	V		V
Appropriate access to audit committee	V	V	V	V	V
Written report on internal control	X	V		V	
Frequency of providing internal audit report	X		X		X
Coercion to change a rating/withdraw finding	V	V	V	V	V
No. of tools used	V	V	V	V	V

"V" indicates factor with significance; "X" indicates factor without significance.

As shown in **Table 3–6**, having appropriate access to the audit committee, without coercion to change a rating assessment or withdraw a finding, and more audit tools or technology used on a typical audit engagement are the most important factors to the perceived contribution of the internal audit activity in every aspect. It is noted that how often a written internal audit report is provided does not matter to the perceived contribution of the internal audit activity, measured in terms of whether it adds value. The provision of a written report on overall internal control for use by the audit committee or senior management does not seem to matter for respondents to perceive whether the internal audit activity adds value. However, it does matter to the perception that the internal audit activity provides a systematic approach to governance, risk management, and control processes.

In 2010, there appears to be a declining trend in sourcing the internal audit activity from outside the organization. The percentage of respondents who did no co-sourcing or outsourcing (57 percent) and outsourced 10 percent or less of their activity (27 percent) totaled 84 percent, compared to 75 percent in 2006. It is intriguing to find that the percentage of co-sourcing or outsourcing the internal audit activity does not have an impact on the perception of value-adding but rather on the effectiveness of the activity, measured in terms of process effectiveness, effective functioning, and sufficient organization status for the activity to be effective.

The results reported here therefore imply that it is more essential to provide appropriate access to the audit committee and foster a working environment without undue or extreme pressure (coercion) to change an audit rating or withdraw audit findings. Having sufficient organizational status and appropriate audit tools, internal auditors are more likely to enhance their positive perception that they add value to the organization.

Chapter 4
Performance Measurement of the Internal Audit Activity

Methods Used to Measure the Performance of the Internal Audit Activity

This section examines the popularity of methods used to measure the performance of the internal audit activity. **Table 4–1** provides the frequency of methods used by the respondents' organizations in 2010 and in five years. It is shown that the top five methods measured in terms of respondents were assessment by percentage of audit plan complete (13.7 percent), acceptance and implementation of recommendations (11.8 percent), assessment by survey or feedback from the board, audit committee, and/or senior management (10.8 percent), assessment by customer/auditee surveys from audited departments (9.1 percent), assurance of sound risk management and internal control (8.3 percent), and reliance by external auditors on the internal audit activity (8.3 percent). The least used internal audit activity performance measurement methods are assessment by absence of regulatory or reputation issues and significant failures (3.8 percent), cycle time from entrance conference to draft report (4.1 percent), and balanced scorecard (4.1 percent). Of the 11,853 respondents, 5.8 percent indicated that they had no formal performance measures for their internal audit activity.

Table 4–1 also indicates that the top five methods used today will continue to be important in the future. In addition, the balanced scorecard method, with the highest percentage (4.1 percent), will gain importance in five years.[4]

To better understand whether the use of performance measurement methods reported in **Table 4–1** are subject to regional and industry variations, further analyses is provided based on classifications by regions and industries. **Table 4–2** presents the results by region, while **Table 4–3** presents the results by industry.

---

[4] It was not clear how respondents interpreted the column "In Five Years." It was intended that they should mark all that they believed would be in use in five years, but it might have been interpreted as asking for only additions to the initial list. The counts suggest that only additions have been marked.

Table 4–1
Ranking of Methods Used to Measure the Performance of Internal Audit Activities — Currently and in Five Years (N=11,853)

Methods	Today count	Today %	In Five Years count	In Five Years %
Percentage of audit plan complete	1,620	13.7	332	2.8
Recommendations accepted/implemented	1,393	11.8	315	2.7
Surveys/feedback from the board, audit committee, and/or senior management	1,279	10.8	443	3.7
Customer/auditee surveys from audited departments	1,075	9.1	443	3.7
Assurance of sound risk management/internal control	980	8.3	381	3.2
Reliance by external auditors on the internal audit activity	979	8.3	294	2.5
Timely closure of audit issues	904	7.6	269	2.3
Completion of mandated coverage	830	7.0	209	1.8
Number of significant audit findings	782	6.6	189	1.6
Budget to actual audit hours	741	6.3	232	2.0
Number of management requests for internal audit assurance or consulting projects	692	5.8	236	2.0
No formal performance measurement of the internal audit activity	687	5.8	102	0.9
Cost savings/avoidance and improvements from recommendations implemented	678	5.7	293	2.5
Cycle time — report turnaround (end of fieldwork to final report)	603	5.1	237	2.0
Balanced scorecard	491	4.1	476	4.0
Cycle time from entrance conference to draft report	491	4.1	231	1.9
Absence of regulatory or reputation issues and significant failures	451	3.8	163	1.4

The top three methods (percentages shown in bold) used by the organizations in each region are ranked to understand whether a difference exists. As indicated in **Table 4–2,** the most commonly used performance measurement methods include assessment by percentage of audit plan complete and acceptance and implementation of recommendations. These findings are consistent with the results shown in **Table 4–1**. Analysis by industry shows that in addition to assessment by percentage of audit plan complete and acceptance and implementation of recommendations, surveys and feedback from the board, audit committee, and/or senior management are measurement methods commonly used by all industries. Based on the results from **Table 4–2** and **Table 4–3**, it appears that there is consensus with regard to how performance of the internal audit activity is measured across regions and industries.

Table 4–2
Regional Comparison of the Methods Currently Used to Measure
the Performance of Internal Audit Activities

Methods		Africa	Asia Pacific	Europe-Central Asia	Latin America/Caribbean	Middle East	United States/Canada	Western Europe	Other	Total*
Balanced scorecard	Col. %	6.2	3.2	3.3	4.4	6.8	2.8	3.3	4.1	4.1
Assurance of sound risk management/internal control	Col. %	6.1	7.8	7.5	6.3	4.9	6.1	7.8	5.7	8.3
Surveys/feedback from the board, audit committee, and/or senior management	Col. %	8.9	9.1	8.0	7.6	6.8	7.9	11.5	7.9	10.8
Customer/auditee surveys from audited departments	Col. %	7.4	7.0	7.1	7.7	8.3	8.6	7.7	6.1	9.1
Recommendations accepted/implemented	Col. %	8.6	8.5	11.8	12.0	9.8	8.6	10.7	12.0	11.8
Cost savings/avoidance and improvements from recommendations implemented	Col. %	4.2	5.9	5.4	5.9	7.1	4.7	3.7	6.1	5.7
Number of management requests for internal audit assurance or consulting projects	Col. %	6.1	5.6	4.8	4.1	4.5	5.3	4.2	5.7	5.8
Reliance by external auditors on the internal audit activity	Col. %	6.8	4.6	4.9	6.2	2.6	8.9	8.2	5.6	8.3
Budget to actual audit hours	Col. %	4.2	4.9	4.8	5.8	5.6	6.7	4.7	4.3	6.3
Percentage of audit plan complete	Col. %	11.1	11.2	11.5	13.5	9.0	11.7	11.4	11.8	13.7
Completion of mandated coverage	Col. %	8.6	6.9	4.8	4.8	7.1	5.7	5.8	5.7	7.0
Cycle time from entrance conference to draft report	Col. %	4.0	3.6	3.7	2.3	4.5	3.4	3.7	3.6	4.1

Table 4–2
Regional Comparison of the Methods Currently Used to Measure the
Performance of Internal Audit Activities (continued)

Methods		Africa	Asia Pacific	Europe-Central Asia	Latin America/Caribbean	Middle East	United States/Canada	Western Europe	Other	Total*
Cycle time — report turnaround (end of fieldwork to final report)	Col. %	4.3	4.4	3.5	3.2	5.3	4.6	4.7	3.6	5.1
Number of significant audit findings	Col. %	6.5	6.3	7.5	6.9	7.1	4.4	4.7	6.9	6.6
Timely closure of audit issues	Col. %	5.4	7.9	**8.0**	6.6	7.1	6.7	4.9	6.9	7.6
Absence of regulatory or reputation issues and significant failures	Col. %	1.7	3.1	3.4	2.8	3.4	3.8	3.0	3.9	3.8
Total after deduction of no formal performance measurement	N	721	2,247	1,550	1,109	266	3,511	3,976	609	
No formal performance measurement of the internal audit activity	N	23	141	73	54	8	156	200	32	

* Total based on rankings of all respondents (see Table 4.1)

Chapter 4: Performance Measurement of the Internal Audit Activity

Table 4–3
Industry Comparison of the Methods Currently Used to Measure the
Performance of Internal Audit Activities

Methods		Financial	Manufacturing & Construction	Public Sector/ Government	Raw Material & Agriculture	Service	Transportation, Communication, Electric, Gas, Sanitary Services	Wholesale & Retail Trade	Other	Total*
Balanced scorecard	Col. %	3.6	3.2	3.4	4.6	2.5	4.4	3.5	3.3	4.1
Assurance of sound risk management/internal control	Col. %	6.9	7.7	6.1	7.3	7.6	6.4	6.2	7.6	8.3
Surveys/feedback from the board, audit committee, and/or senior management	Col. %	9.1	9.4	8.2	9.9	9.5	8.9	8.8	9.7	10.8
Customer/auditee surveys from audited departments	Col. %	7.3	7.4	9.3	7.1	8.3	7.6	7.0	7.9	9.1
Recommendations accepted/implemented	Col. %	9.2	9.8	11.8	8.9	10.5	10.3	9.9	10.5	11.8
Cost savings/avoidance and improvements from recommendations implemented	Col. %	3.6	6.0	4.1	6.9	5.3	5.3	7.6	3.9	5.7
Number of management requests for internal audit assurance or consulting projects	Col. %	4.1	5.1	5.4	5.2	5.8	5.4	5.4	4.8	5.8
Reliance by external auditors on the internal audit activity	Col. %	8.0	6.1	5.4	5.6	7.8	7.1	6.5	6.4	8.3
Budget to actual audit hours	Col. %	5.8	4.2	5.5	5.5	5.1	5.4	4.8	5.6	6.3
Percentage of audit plan complete	Col. %	12.3	11.7	11.8	11.8	10.3	11.4	10.5	10.8	13.7
Completion of mandated coverage	Col. %	6.3	6.6	5.5	5.0	5.7	5.5	5.9	5.1	7.0
Cycle time from entrance conference to draft report	Col. %	3.5	3.2	4.4	2.9	2.9	3.6	3.7	4.3	4.1

A Component of the CBOK Study

Measuring Internal Auditing's Value

Table 4–3
Industry Comparison of the Methods Currently Used to Measure the Performance of Internal Audit Activities (continued)

Methods		Financial	Manufacturing & Construction	Public Sector/ Government	Raw Material & Agriculture	Service	Transportation, Communication, Electric, Gas, Sanitary Services	Wholesale & Retail Trade	Other	Total *
Cycle time — report turnaround (end of fieldwork to final report)	Col. %	4.4	4.6	4.2	4.3	3.4	4.8	4.0	4.5	5.1
Number of significant audit findings	Col. %	5.3	5.8	5.9	5.5	5.5	5.5	6.4	5.8	6.6
Timely closure of audit issues	Col. %	6.2	7.0	5.8	6.3	6.5	6.5	7.2	7.2	7.6
Absence of regulatory or reputation issues and significant failures	Col. %	4.4	2.2	3.0	3.2	3.3	2.1	2.7	2.7	3.8
Total after deduction of no formal performance measurement	N	4,469	2,309	1,285	695	1,786	1,841	628	976	
No formal performance measurement	N	179	142	56	26	114	76	39	55	

* Total based on rankings of all respondents (see Table 4.1)

Summary and Implications

The analysis on common performance measures of an internal audit activity indicates that the top ranked methods currently used include assessment by percentage of audit plan completed, acceptance and implementation of recommendations, surveys/feedback from the board/audit committee/senior management, customer/auditee surveys from audited departments, assurance of sound risk management, and reliance by external auditors on the internal audit activity. The least used internal audit activity performance measurement methods are assessment by absence of regulatory or reputation issues and significant failures, cycle time from entrance conference to draft report, and balanced scorecard. It is worth noting that the top ranked methods used today will continue to be important in the future. In addition, the balanced scorecard and assurance of sound risk management/internal control methods are expected to gain importance in five years' time. Regional and industry comparisons regarding the performance measures of the internal audit activity show no significant differences.

Chapter 5
Performance Measurement Methods and Perceived Contributions

The methods used to measure an internal audit activity's performance, in general, will affect its efforts and focus on different audit activities, and thus its perceived contributions to the organization. To determine whether there is a relationship between the performance measurement methods currently used by the internal audit activities and their perceived contributions, a correlation analysis between the performance measurement methods and perceived contribution is presented. **Table 5–1** provides the resulting correlation coefficients for all variables.

It shows that, for each performance measurement method, the correlations with different value statements are fairly consistent. The method with the highest correlation is percentage of audit plan complete (M10), with most coefficients close to 0.7. This association reflects the basic requirement of an internal audit activity to fulfill its annual audit plan.

The other two methods with high correlation are recommendations accepted/implemented (M5) and surveys/feedback from the board, audit committee, and/or senior management (M3), with all of the coefficients above 0.6. The methods are more outcome-oriented and indicative of the internal audit activity's contribution to organizational process improvements.

In addition, there are three methods with correlation coefficients above 0.5: assurance of sound risk management/internal control (M2), customer/auditee surveys from audited departments (M4), and reliance by external auditors on the internal audit activity (M8). Similarly, these methods are used to measure the internal audit activity's outcome and its usefulness to the auditee and the organization.

For the remaining performance measurement methods, the correlation coefficients lie between 0.3 and 0.5. These numbers indicate a weaker association between each of these methods and the value statements. Among these methods, M12, M13, and M15 are more process-oriented; M6 and M9 measure financial benefits/budget controls; and M7 indicates the usage of internal audit services.

In summary, the performance measurement methods used by the internal audit activities are associated with their perceived contributions. While the more outcome-oriented methods show a higher correlation with the value statements, the remaining methods also have medium association with these statements. The results imply that although it is important for internal auditors to use their resources efficiently (measured by the process-oriented performance indicators), the outcome of their work is imperative for the internal audit activities to provide value to the organizations.

Table 5–1
Pearson Correlation between Value Statements and Performance Measurement Methods*

Performance Measurement Method**	A2	A10	A11	A3	A4	A5	A1	A6	A7	A8	A13	A14	A9	A12	A15
M1	.372	.362	.360	.381	.372	.378	.363	.365	.378	.378	.378	.371	.376	.370	.373
M2	.531	.523	.525	.542	.536	.539	.527	.538	.537	.518	.524	.520	.531	.527	.524
M3	.608	.610	.613	.614	.617	.620	.614	.612	.617	.616	.609	.607	.621	.613	.615
M4	.555	.555	.556	.564	.564	.560	.561	.558	.565	.557	.562	.560	.561	.558	.567
M5	.642	.636	.633	.643	.641	.639	.640	.639	.643	.624	.641	.635	.646	.641	.634
M6	.439	.426	.427	.436	.432	.438	.421	.443	.435	.418	.428	.431	.433	.427	.427
M7	.440	.435	.436	.442	.439	.447	.434	.442	.446	.434	.438	.439	.441	.435	.440
M8	.530	.529	.530	.536	.539	.527	.536	.532	.532	.529	.516	.521	.537	.535	.532
M9	.454	.455	.455	.459	.458	.462	.457	.457	.466	.468	.458	.457	.457	.457	.461
M10	.696	.697	.699	.696	.698	.688	.699	.689	.701	.694	.696	.692	.697	.697	.693
M11	.479	.480	.480	.488	.483	.491	.482	.484	.492	.489	.483	.485	.489	.483	.482
M12	.361	.362	.362	.367	.365	.370	.361	.364	.374	.362	.378	.369	.370	.367	.372
M13	.408	.404	.407	.414	.411	.409	.406	.411	.418	.412	.415	.409	.416	.411	.415
M14	.468	.461	.462	.465	.462	.472	.458	.467	.474	.458	.469	.468	.461	.460	.455
M15	.505	.494	.495	.506	.503	.508	.497	.506	.514	.502	.502	.502	.506	.502	.504
M16	.348	.342	.351	.352	.351	.353	.348	.357	.356	.347	.341	.346	.354	.357	.352
M17	.408	.407	.411	.388	.397	.387	.404	.401	.386	.365	.389	.401	.383	.400	.393

* 2-tailed Chi-square test, significance level =0.000 for all items. The number of respondents varies across the 15 value statements (see Table 2-1).

** M1: Balanced scorecard; M2: Assurance of sound risk management/internal control; M3: Surveys/feedback from the board, audit committee, and/or senior management; M4: Customer/auditee surveys from audited departments; M5: Recommendations accepted/implemented; M6: Cost savings/avoidance and improvements from recommendations implemented; M7: Number of management requests for internal audit assurance or consulting projects; M8: Reliance by external auditors on the internal audit activity; M9: Budget to actual audit hours; M10: Percentage of audit plan complete; M11: Completion of mandated coverage; M12: Cycle time from entrance conference to draft report; M13: Cycle time — report turnaround; M14: Number of significant audit findings; M15: Timely closure of audit issues; M16: Absence of regulatory or reputation issues and significant failures; M17: No formal performance measurement.

Chapter 6
Audit Activities Performed and Perceived Contributions

In general, when an internal audit activity performs more services, its perceived contribution is expected to be higher. To determine whether there is such a relationship, a correlation analysis between the number of audit activities performed and the respondents' level of agreement with the value statements is presented. While not tabulated, the results show that the level of agreement with each value statement is generally positively associated with the number of audit services performed.[5]

The 2010 survey question on internal audit activities performed includes 25 items. These items were classified into three groups: internal control, risk management, and corporate governance (**Table 6–1**) to be able to examine how the extent of different services affects the value statements, A2, A3, A4, and A5.

Table 6–1
Classification of Internal Audit Activities Performed

Group 1: Internal Control
2. Audits of compliance with regulatory code (including privacy) requirements
3. Evaluating effectiveness of control systems (using COSO, COBIT, etc., frameworks)
9. Operational audits
10. Project management assurance/audits of major projects
12. Security assessments and investigations
14. Disaster recovery testing and support
15. Investigations of fraud and irregularities
19. Quality/ISO audits
20. External audit assistance
21. Management audits
22. Facilitating risk/control/compliance training and education for organization personnel
23. Auditing of outsourced operations
24. Migration to International Financial Reporting Standards (IFRS)
25. Implementation of Extensible Business Reporting Language (XBRL)
Group 2: Risk Management
4. Business viability (going-concern) assessments
7. Audits of enterprise risk management processes

---

[5] 2-tailed Chi-square test, significance level =0.000 for all items.

Table 6–1
Classification of Internal Audit Activities Performed (continued)

- 8. Auditing of financial risks
- 11. Auditing of information risks
- 13. Auditing of IT/ICT risks

Group 3: Corporate Governance

- 1. Corporate governance reviews
- 5. Due diligence reviews for corporate acquisitions/mergers, etc.
- 6. Ethics audits
- 16. Reviews addressing linkage of strategy and company performance (e.g., balanced scorecard)
- 17. Executive compensation assessments
- 18. Social and sustainability (corporate social responsibility, environmental) audits

Table 6–2 shows that the relationships between different types of audit services performed and the four value statements are low. The correlation for statement A2 (add value) with internal control audit activities is higher than those with the other two groups. This implies that a higher proportion of internal audit activities' perceived contribution is derived from providing internal control audit activities.

Table 6–2
Pearson Correlation between Value Statements and Internal Audit Activities Performed*

Audit Services Performed	A2: Add value	A3: Risk management	A4: Internal controls	A5: Governance
Internal control	**.150**	.206	**.204**	.216
Risk management	.123	**.254**	.212	.210
Governance	.103	.188	.114	**.286**

* 2-tailed Chi-squared test, significance level =0.000 for all items.

In addition, for the value statements on risk management (A3) and governance (A5), their correlations (0.254 and 0.286) with respective audit activities are the highest among the three value statements on bringing systematic approaches to risk management, internal control, and governance processes. These relationships are consistent with the expectation that the efforts in performing risk management or governance services have more of an effect on the respondents' perceived contribution of their internal audit activities to the related processes.

In summary, the scope of internal audit activities is positively associated with their perceived contribution. While the relationships between different types of audit services performed and the four value statements are low, there is higher correlation between internal control-related audit activities and the perceived contribution. The audit activities related to governance and risk management also have a higher correlation with the internal audit activities' perceived contribution to these processes.

Chapter 7
Conclusion

Analysis of survey results discussed in this report indicates that most respondents believe their internal audit activities are adding value to their organizations. Both independence and objectivity are viewed as key factors. While most internal audit functions see themselves as contributing to controls, they do not to the same extent perceive themselves as contributing to risk management or governance. The results from regional comparisons indicate that there are significant differences across the seven regions in terms of internal audit activities' perceived contribution to their organizations. Based on the results from industrial comparison, the industry groups with the top three levels of agreement are service, financial, and raw material and agriculture. However, since most industry groups are spread across different regions, the above results represent, to some extent, the averaging effect of internal audit activities from different regions. In addition, there is no industry that is consistently ranked as the lowest among the industry groups.

The most important factors to the perceived contribution of an internal audit activity in every aspect are 1) having appropriate access to the audit committee; 2) without coercion to change a rating assessment or withdraw a finding, and 3) more audit tools or technology used on a typical audit engagement. Compared to 2006, there appears to be a declining trend in sourcing the internal audit activity from outside the organization. The percentage of co-sourcing or outsourcing the internal audit activity does not have an impact on the perception of value-adding but rather on the effectiveness of the internal audit activity, measured in terms of process effectiveness, effective functioning, and sufficient organization status.

The results imply that it is more essential to provide appropriate access to the audit committee and foster a working environment without undue or extreme pressure (coercion) to change an audit rating or withdraw audit findings. Having sufficient organizational status and appropriate audit tools, internal auditors are more likely to enhance their positive perception that they add value to the organization.

Most frequently used performance methods for the internal audit activity include 1) assessment by percentage of the audit plan completed; 2) acceptance and implementation of recommendations; 3) surveys/feedback from the board/audit committee/senior management; 4) customer/auditee surveys from audited departments; 5) assurance of sound risk management; and 6) reliance by external auditors on the internal audit activity. The balanced scorecard and assurance of sound risk management/internal control methods are expected to gain importance as internal audit activity performance methods in the coming years.

In addition, the methods used to measure the performance of internal audit activities are associated with their perceived contributions. The more outcome-oriented methods show a higher correlation with the value statements.

The IIA's Global Internal Audit Survey — Questions

The entire IIA Global Internal Audit Survey, including question and answer options and glossary, may be downloaded from The IIARF's website (www.theiia.org/research). The following table provides an overview of the questions and groups that answered the specific questions. In addition, the table indicates in which report the survey data were (mostly) used.

Question #	Section and Description of Question	CAE	Service Provider Partner	Service Provider Non-partner	Practitioners (staff levels in-house and at-service providers)	Academics and Others	Data Used in Report
Personal/Background Information							
1a	How long have you been a member of The IIA?	X	X	X	X	X	I & V
1b	Please select your local IIA.	X	X	X	X	X	I & V
1c	Please select the location in which you primarily practice professionally.	X	X	X	X	X	I & V
2a	Your age.	X	X	X	X	X	I & V
2b	Your gender.	X	X	X	X	X	I & V
3	Your highest level of formal education (not certification) completed.	X	X	X	X	X	I & V
4	Your academic major(s).	X	X	X	X	X	I & V
5a	Do you work for a professional firm that provides internal audit services?	X	X	X	X	X	I & V
5b	Your position in the organization.	X	X	X	X	X	I & V
6	Your professional certification(s) (please mark all that apply).	X	X	X	X	X	I & V
7	Specify your professional experience (please mark all that apply).	X	X	X	X	X	I & V
8	How many total years have you been the CAE or equivalent at your current organization and previous organizations you have worked for?	X					I
9	Where do you administratively report (direct line) in your organization?	X					I & V
10	Do you receive at least 40 hours of formal training per year?	X	X	X	X		I & V

Question #	Section and Description of Question	CAE	Service Provider Partner	Service Provider Non-partner	Practitioners (staff levels in-house and at-service providers)	Academics and Others	Data Used in Report
Your Organization							
11	The type of organization for which you currently work.	X	X	X	X		I
12	The broad industry classification of the organization for which you work or provide internal audit services.	X	X	X	X		I
13a	Size of the entire organization for which you work as of December 31, 2009, or the end of the last fiscal year (total employees).	X	X	X	X		I & V
13b	Total assets in U.S. dollars.	X	X	X	X		I & V
13c	Total revenue or budget if government or not-for-profit in U.S. dollars.	X	X	X	X		I & V
14	Is your organization (local, regional, international)?	X	X	X	X		I & V
Internal Audit Activity							
15	How long has your organization's internal audit activity been in place?	X			X		I, III, & V
16	Which of the following exist in your organization (e.g., corporate governance code; internal audit charter)?	X			X		I, III, & V
17a	Who is involved in appointing the chief audit executive (CAE) or equivalent?	X					I & III
17b	Who is involved in appointing the internal audit service provider?	X	X				I & III
18	Who contributes to the evaluation of your performance?	X					I & III
19	Is there an audit committee or equivalent in your organization?	X					I, III, & V
20a	Number of formal audit committee meetings held in the last fiscal year.	X					I & III
20b	Number of audit committee meetings you were invited to attend (entirely or in part) during the last fiscal year.	X					I & III
20c	Do you meet or talk with the audit committee/chairman in addition to regularly scheduled meetings?	X					I & III
20d	Do you meet with the audit committee/oversight committee/chairman in private executive sessions during regularly scheduled meetings?	X					I & III

The IIA's Global Internal Audit Survey — Questions

Question #	Section and Description of Question	CAE	Service Provider Partner	Service Provider Non-partner	Practitioners (staff levels in-house and at-service providers)	Academics and Others	Data Used in Report
21a	Do you believe that you have appropriate access to the audit committee?	X	X				I & III
21b	Do you prepare a written report on overall internal control for use by the audit committee or senior management? Do you prepare a written report on overall internal control for use by the audit committee or senior management? How often do you provide a report?	X	X				I & III
21c	Does your organization provide a report on internal control in its annual report?	X	X				I & III
21d	Which of the following are included in the annual report item on internal control?	X	X				I & III
21e	Who signs the report on internal controls?	X	X				I & III
22	How does your organization measure the performance of the internal audit activity?	X					I, III, & V
23a	How frequently do you update the audit plan?	X					I & III
23b	How do you establish your audit plan?	X					I, III, & V
24a	What is your IT/ICT audit strategy?	X					I, III, & V
24b	What is the nature of your internal audit activity's technology strategy?	X					I, III, & V
25a	What is the number of organizations to which you (as an individual) currently provide internal audit services?			X			I & III
25b	Please indicate your agreement with the following statements as they relate to your current organization or organizations that you audit.	X					I, III, & V
Staffing							
26a	Is your organization offering any special incentives to hire/retain internal audit professionals?	X					I & III
26b	What sources does your organization use to recruit audit staff?	X					I & III
26c	Does your organization use college interns/undergraduate placements?	X					I, III, & V
26d	What is your primary reason for employing college interns/undergraduate placements?	X					I, III, & V

Measuring Internal Auditing's Value

Question #	Section and Description of Question	CAE	Service Provider Partner	Service Provider Non-partner	Practitioners (staff levels in-house and at-service providers)	Academics and Others	Data Used in Report
27	What methods do you use to make up for staff vacancies?	X					I & III
28	What methods is your organization employing to compensate for missing skill sets?	X					I & III
29	What percentage of your internal audit activities is currently co-sourced/outsourced?	X					I & III
30a	How do you anticipate that your budget for co-sourced/outsourced activities will change in the next five years?	X					I & III
30b	How do you anticipate that your permanent staff levels will change in the next five years?	X					I, III, & V
31	What method of staff evaluation do you use?	X					I & III
Internal Audit Standards							
32	Does your organization use the *Standards*? If you are a service provider, do you use the *Standards* for internal audits of your clients?	X	X				II, III, & V
33	If your internal audit activity follows any of the *Standards*, please indicate if the guidance provided by these standards is adequate for your internal audit activity and if you believe your organization complies with the *Standards*.	X	X				II, III, & V
33a	Do you believe that the guidance provided by the *Standards* is adequate for internal auditing?					X	II, III, & V
34	Your organization is in compliance.	X					II, III, & V
35	What are the reasons for not using the *Standards* in whole or in part?	X	X				II, III, & V
36	Does your internal audit activity have a quality assessment and improvement program in place in accordance with Standard 1300?	X					II, III, & V
37a	When was your internal audit activity last subject to a formal external quality assessment in accordance with Standard 1312?	X					II, III, & V
37b	Why has such a review not been undertaken?	X					II, III, & V

Question #	Section and Description of Question	CAE	Service Provider Partner	Service Provider Non-partner	Practitioners (staff levels in-house and at-service providers)	Academics and Others	Data Used in Report
37c	As a provider of internal audit services, are your internal audit processes subjected to external quality assessments as specified in Standard 1312?		X				II, III, & V
38	For your internal audit activity, which of the following is part of your internal audit quality assessment and improvement program?	X					II, III, & V
Audit Activities							
39	Please indicate whether your internal audit activity performs (or is anticipated to perform) the following:	X	X	X	X		I, III, & V
40a	Do you usually provide a form of opinion of the audit subject area in individual internal audit reports?	X	X	X	X		I & III
40b	Do you usually provide an overall rating (such as satisfactory/unsatisfactory) of the audit subject area in individual internal audit reports?	X	X	X	X		I & III
40c	Have you ever been subject to coercion (extreme pressure) to change a rating or assessment or to withdraw a finding in an internal audit report?	X	X	X	X		I & III
41	After the release of an audit report in the organization, who has the primary responsibility for reporting findings to senior management?	X	X	X	X		I & III
42	After the release of an audit report with findings that need corrective action, who has the primary responsibility to monitor that corrective action has been taken?	X	X	X	X		I & III
Tools, Skills, and Competencies							
43a	Indicate the extent the internal audit activity uses or plans to use the following audit tools or techniques on a typical audit engagement.	X	X	X	X		II, III, & V
43b	What other tools and techniques are you currently using or planning to use (indicate if proprietary)?	X	X	X	X		II, III, & V
44	Please mark the five most important of the following behavioral skills for each professional staff level to perform their work.	X	X			X	II, III, & V
44a	Please indicate the importance of the following behavioral skills for you to perform your work at your position in the organization				X	X	II, III, & V
45	Please mark the five most important of the following technical skills for each level of professional staff to perform their work.	X	X			X	II, III, & V

Question #	Section and Description of Question	CAE	Service Provider Partner	Service Provider Non-partner	Practitioners (staff levels in-house and at-service providers)	Academics and Others	Data Used in Report
45a	Please indicate the importance of the following technical skills for you to perform your work at your position in the organization.			X	X		II, III, & V
46	Please mark the five most important of the following competencies for each level of professional rank to perform their work.	X	X			X	II, III, & V
46a	Please indicate the importance of the following competencies for you to perform your work at your position in the organization.			X	X		II, III, & V
46b	How important are the following areas of knowledge for satisfactory performance of your job in your position in the organization?			X	X		II, III, & V
46c	Are there other areas of knowledge that you consider essential?			X	X		II, III, & V
Emerging Issues							
47	Do you perceive likely changes in the following roles of the internal audit activity over the next five years?	X	X	X	X	X	IV & V
48	Please indicate if the following statements apply to your organization now, in the next five years, or will not apply in the foreseeable future.	X	X	X	X		IV & V

The IIA's Global Internal Audit Survey — Glossary

This glossary was made available to respondents when they participated in the survey.

Add Value
Value is provided by improving opportunities to achieve organizational objectives, identifying operational improvement, and/or reducing risk exposure through both assurance and consulting services.

Assurance Services
An objective examination of evidence for the purpose of providing an independent assessment on governance, risk management, and control processes for the organization. Examples may include financial, performance, compliance, system security, and due diligence engagements.

Audit Risk
The risk of reaching invalid audit conclusions and/or providing faulty advice based on the audit work conducted.

Auditee
The subsidiary, business unit, department, group, or other established subdivision of an organization that is the subject of an assurance engagement.

Board
A board is an organization's governing body, such as a board of directors, supervisory board, head of an agency or legislative body, board of governors or trustees of a nonprofit organization, or any other designated body of the organization, including the audit committee to whom the chief audit executive may functionally report.

Business Process
The set of connected activities linked with each other for the purpose of achieving one or more business objectives.

Chief Audit Executive
Chief audit executive is a senior position within the organization responsible for internal audit activities. Normally, this would be the internal audit director. In the case where internal audit activities are obtained from external service providers, the chief audit executive is the person responsible for overseeing the service contract and the overall quality assurance of these activities, reporting to senior management and the board regarding internal audit activities, and follow-up of engagement results. The term also includes titles such as general auditor, head of internal audit, chief internal auditor, and inspector general.

Code of Ethics
The Code of Ethics of The Institute of Internal Auditors (IIA) are Principles relevant to the profession and practice of internal auditing, and Rules of Conduct that describe behavior expected of internal auditors. The Code of Ethics applies to both parties and entities that provide internal audit services.

The purpose of the Code of Ethics is to promote an ethical culture in the global profession of internal auditing.

Compliance
Adherence to policies, plans, procedures, laws, regulations, contracts, or other requirements.

Consulting Services
Advisory and related client service activities, the nature and scope of which are agreed with the client, are intended to add value and improve an organization's governance, risk management, and control processes without the internal auditor assuming management responsibility. Examples include counsel, advice, facilitation, and training.

Control
Any action taken by management, the board, and other parties to manage risk and increase the likelihood that established objectives and goals will be achieved. Management plans, organizes, and directs the performance of sufficient actions to provide reasonable assurance that objectives and goals will be achieved.

Customer
The subsidiary, business unit, department, group, individual, or other established subdivision of an organization that is the subject of a consulting engagement.

Engagement
A specific internal audit assignment, task, or review activity, such as an internal audit, control self-assessment review, fraud examination, or consultancy. An engagement may include multiple tasks or activities designed to accomplish a specific set of related objectives.

Enterprise Risk Management — See Risk Management

External Auditor
A registered public accounting firm, hired by the organization's board or executive management, to perform a financial statement audit providing assurance for which the firm issues a written attestation report that expresses an opinion about whether the financial statements are fairly presented in accordance with applicable Generally Accepted Accounting Principles.

Framework
A body of guiding principles that form a template against which organizations can evaluate a multitude of business practices. These principles are comprised of various concepts, values, assumptions, and practices intended to provide a yardstick against which an organization can assess or evaluate a particular structure, process, or environment or a group of practices or procedures.

Fraud
Any illegal act characterized by deceit, concealment, or violation of trust. These acts are not dependent upon the threat of violence or physical force. Frauds are perpetrated by parties and organizations

to obtain money, property, or services; to avoid payment or loss of services; or to secure personal or business advantage.

Governance

The combination of processes and structures implemented by the board to inform, direct, manage, and monitor the activities of the organization toward the achievement of its objectives.

Independence

The freedom from conditions that threaten objectivity or the appearance of objectivity. Such threats to objectivity must be managed at the individual auditor, engagement, functional, and organizational levels.

Internal Audit Activity

A department, division, team of consultants, or other practitioner(s) that provides independent, objective assurance and consulting services designed to add value and improve an organization's operations. The internal audit activity helps an organization accomplish its objectives by bringing a systematic, disciplined approach to evaluate and improve the effectiveness of governance, risk management, and control processes.

Internal Audit Charter

The internal audit charter is a formal document that defines the internal audit activity's purpose, authority, and responsibility. The internal audit charter establishes the internal audit activity's position within the organization; authorizes access to records, personnel, and physical properties relevant to the performance of engagements; and defines the scope of internal audit activities.

Internal Control

A process, effected by an entity's board of directors, management, and other personnel, designed to provide reasonable assurance regarding the achievement of objectives in the following categories:

- ☐ Effectiveness and efficiency of operations.
- ☐ Reliability of financial reporting.
- ☐ Compliance with applicable laws and regulations.

International Professional Practices Framework

The conceptual framework that organizes the authoritative guidance promulgated by The IIA. Authoritative Guidance is comprised of two categories — (1) mandatory and (2) strongly recommended.

IT/ICT

Information technology/information communication technology.

Monitoring

A process that assesses the presence and functioning of governance, risk management, and control over time.

Objectivity

An unbiased mental attitude that allows internal auditors to perform engagements in such a manner that they have an honest belief in their work product and that no significant quality compromises are made. Objectivity requires internal auditors not to subordinate their judgment on audit matters to others.

Risk

The possibility of an event occurring that will have an impact on the achievement of objectives. Risk is measured in terms of impact and likelihood.

Risk Assessment

The identification and analysis (typically in terms of impact and likelihood) of relevant risks to the achievement of an organization's objectives, forming a basis for determining how the risks should be managed.

Risk Management

A process to identify, assess, manage, and control potential events or situations to provide reasonable assurance regarding the achievement of the organization's objectives.

Service Provider

A person or firm, outside of the organization, who provides assurance and/or consulting services to an organization.

Standard

A professional pronouncement promulgated by the Internal Audit Standards Board that delineates the requirements for performing a broad range of internal audit activities, and for evaluating internal audit performance.

Strategy

Refers to how management plans to achieve the organization's objectives.

Technology-based Audit Techniques

Any automated audit tool, such as generalized audit software, test data generators, computerized audit programs, specialized audit utilities, and computer-assisted audit techniques (CAATs).

The IIA Research Foundation Sponsor Recognition

The vision of The IIA Research Foundation is to understand, shape, and advance the global profession of internal auditing by initiating and sponsoring intelligence gathering, innovative research, and knowledge-sharing in a timely manner. As a separate, tax-exempt organization, The Foundation does not receive funding from IIA membership dues but depends on contributions from individuals and organizations, and from IIA chapters and institutes, to move our programs forward. We also would not be able to function without our valuable volunteers. To that end, we thank the following:

The William G. Bishop III, CIA, Memorial Fund

DIAMOND LEVEL
The Institute of Internal Auditors (IIA)

EMERALD LEVEL
William L. Taylor
IIA–Central Illinois Chapter
IIA–Dallas Chapter
IIA–New York Chapter

RUBY LEVEL
Jewel and Dennis K. Beran, CIA, CCSA
Mary Bishop
John J. Flaherty, CIA
Anthony J. Ridley, CIA
Patricia E. Scipio, CIA
IIA–Dallas Chapter
IIA–New York Chapter
IIA–Palmetto Chapter
IIA–Pittsburgh Chapter
IIA–Washington, DC Chapter

FRIEND LEVEL
Andrew J. Dahle, CIA
John M. Polarinakis, CIA
IIA–Downeast Maine Chapter
IIA–Madison Chapter
IIA–Phoenix Chapter
IIA–Triad Chapter
IIA–Wichita Chapter

DONOR LEVEL
Abdulrahman AlSughayer
Augusto Baeta
Audley L. Bell, CIA
Jewel and Dennis K. Beran, CIA, CCSA
Toby Bishop
LeRoy E. Bookal, CIA
Mahmood Al-Hassan Bukhari
Judith K. Burke, CCSA
Richard F. Chambers, CIA, CCSA, CGAP
Michael J. Corcoran
Nicolette Creatore
Julia Ann Disner, CIA, CFSA
Edward M. Dudley, CIA
Gaston L. Gianni, Jr., CGAP
Stephen D. Goepfert, CIA
Al and Kendra Holzinger
Cynthia Huysman
Howard J. Johnson, CIA
Thomas A. Johnson, CIA
Claude Joseph
Nathania Kasman
Carman L. Lapointe, CIA, CCSA
Jens Lay
Lorna Linton
Susan B. Lione, CIA, CCSA, CFSA, CGAP
Mary Lueckemeyer
David J. MacCabe, CIA, CGAP
Stacy Mantzaris, CIA, CCSA, CGAP

Joseph P. McGinley
Betty L. McPhilimy, CIA
Guenther Meggeneder, CIA
Patricia K. Miller, CIA
Anthony Minor, CIA
James A. Molzahn, CIA
Donald J. Nelson, CIA
Frank M. O'Brien, CIA
Basil H. Pflumm, CIA
David N. Polansky
Charity A. Prentice, CIA, CCSA, CGAP
Tabitha Price

Robert John Serocki, CIA, CCSA
Hugh E. Spellman
Frederick H. Tesch, CIA, CFSA
Archie R. Thomas, CIA
Don Trobaugh, CIA, CFSA
Bonnie L. Ulmer
Dominique Vincenti, CIA
Douglas E. Ziegenfuss, PhD, CIA, CCSA
IIA–Baltimore Chapter
IIA–El Paso Chapter
IIA–Nisqually Chapter
IIA–Tallahassee Chapter
Other Research Sponsors

Other Research Sponsors

Research Sponsors

IIA–Chicago Chapter
IIA–Houston Chapter
IIA Netherlands
IIA–Philadelphia Chapter

Principal Partners

Strategic Partners
ACL Services Ltd.
CCH® TeamMate

Partners
CaseWare IDEA Inc.
Ernst & Young LLP
PricewaterhouseCoopers, LLP

Visionary Circle

The Family of Lawrence B. Sawyer

Chairman's Circle

Stephen D. Goepfert, CIA
Michael J. Head, CIA
Patricia E. Scipio, CIA
Paul J. Sobel, CIA

ExxonMobil Corporation
Itau Unibanco Holding SA
JCPenney Company
Lockheed Martin Corporation
Southern California Edison Company

Diamond Donor

IIA–Central Ohio Chapter
IIA–New York Chapter
IIA–San Jose Chapter

The IIA Research Foundation Board of Trustees

President: Patricia E. Scipio, CIA, *PricewaterhouseCoopers LLP*
Vice President-Strategy: Mark J. Pearson, CIA, *Boise Inc.*
Vice President-Research: Philip E. Flora, CIA, CCSA, *FloBiz & Associates, LLC*
Vice President-Development: Wayne G. Moore, CIA, *Wayne Moore Consulting*
Treasurer: Stephen W. Minder, CIA, *YCN Group LLC*
Secretary: Douglas Ziegenfuss, PhD, CIA, CCSA, *Old Dominion University*

Neil Aaron, *The McGraw-Hill Companies*
Richard J. Anderson, CFSA, *DePaul University*
Urton L. Anderson, PhD, CIA, CCSA, CFSA, CGAP, *University of Texas-Austin*
Sten Bjelke, CIA, *IIA Sweden*
Michael J. Head, CIA, *TD Ameritrade Holding Corporation*
James A. LaTorre, *PricewaterhouseCoopers LLP*
Marjorie Maguire-Krupp, CIA, CFSA, *Coastal Empire Consulting*
Leen Paape, CIA, *Nyenrode Business University*
Jeffrey Perkins, CIA, *TransUnion LLC*
Edward C. Pitts, *Avago Technologies*
Michael F. Pryal, CIA, *Federal Signal Corporation*
Larry E. Rittenberg, PhD, CIA, *University of Wisconsin*
Carolyn Saint, CIA, *Lowe's Companies, Inc.*
Mark L. Salamasick, CIA, *University of Texas at Dallas*
Susan D. Ulrey, CIA, *KPMG LLP*
Jacqueline K. Wagner, CIA, *Ernst & Young LLP*
Shi Xian, *Nanjing Audit University*

The IIA Research Foundation Committee of Research and Education Advisors

Chairman: Philip E. Flora, CIA, CCSA, *FloBiz & Associates, LLC*
Vice-chairman: Urton L. Anderson, PhD, CIA, CCSA, CFSA, CGAP, *University of Texas-Austin*

Members

George R. Aldhizer III, PhD, CIA, *Wake Forest University*
Lalbahadur Balkaran, CIA
Kevin W. Barthold, CPA, *City of San Antonio*
Thomas J. Beirne, CFSA, *The AES Corporation*
Audley L. Bell, CIA, *Habitat for Humanity International*
Toby Bishop, *Deloitte FAS LLP*
Sezer Bozkus, CIA, CFSA, *KPMG LLP*
John K. Brackett, CFSA, *RSM McGladrey, Inc.*
Adil S. Buhariwalla, CIA, *Emirates Airlines*
Thomas J. Clooney, CIA, CCSA, *KPMG LLP*
Jean Coroller
Mary Christine Dobrovich, *Jefferson Wells International*
Susan Page Driver, CIA, *Texas General Land Office*
Donald A. Espersen, CIA, *despersen & associates*
Randall R. Fernandez, CIA, *C-Force, Inc.*
John C. Gazlay, CPA, CCSA
Dan B. Gould, CIA
Ulrich Hahn, CIA, CCSA, CGAP
John C. Harris, CIA, *Aspen Holdings/FirstComp Insurance Company*
Sabrina B. Hearn, CIA, *University of Alabama System*
Katherine E. Homer, *Ernst & Young LLP*
Peter M. Hughes, PhD, CIA, *Orange County*
David J. MacCabe, CIA, CGAP
Gary R. McGuire, CIA, *Lennox International Inc.*
John D. McLaughlin, *LECG, LLC*
Steven S. Mezzio, CIA, CCSA, CFSA, *Resources Global Professionals*
Deborah L. Munoz, CIA, *CalPortland Company*
Frank M. O'Brien, CIA, *Olin Corporation*
Michael L. Piazza, *Professional Development Institute*
Amy Jane Prokopetz, CCSA, *Farm Credit Canada*
Mark R. Radde, CIA, *Resources Global Professionals*
Vito Raimondi, CIA, *Zurich Financial Services NA*
Sandra W. Shelton, PhD, *DePaul University*
Linda Yanta, CIA, *Eskom*